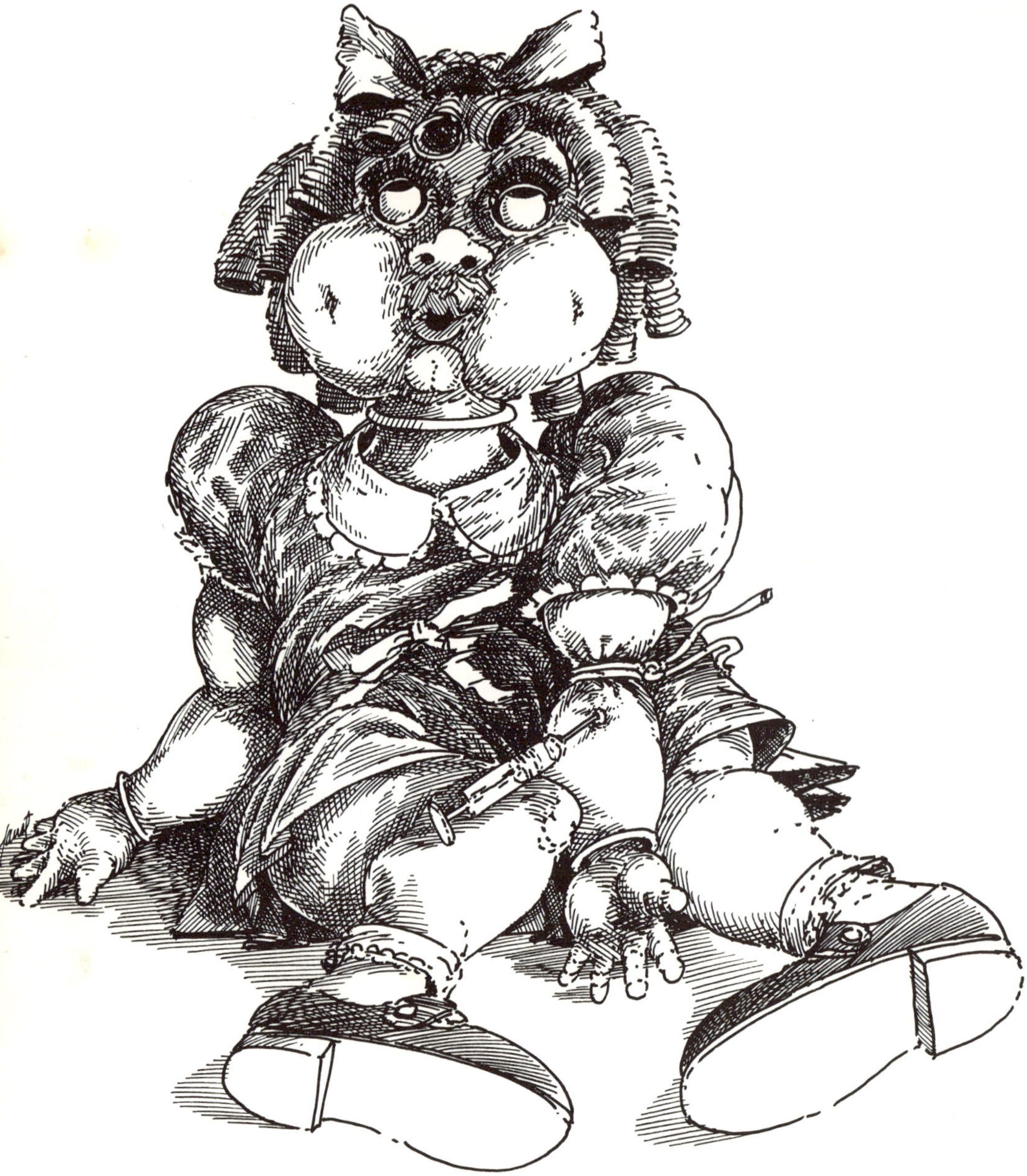

The Underground Sketchbook of Jan Faust

Dover Publications, Inc.
New York

Copyright © 1971 by Dover Publications, Inc.
All rights reserved under Pan American and International Copyright Conventions.

Published in Canada by General Publishing Company, Ltd., 30 Lesmill Road, Don Mills, Toronto, Ontario.
Published in the United Kingdom by Constable and Company, Ltd., 10 Orange Street, London WC 2.

The Underground Sketchbook of Jan Faust is a new work, first published by Dover Publications, Inc., in 1971.

DOVER *Pictorial Archive* SERIES

This book belongs to the Dover Pictorial Archive Series. Up to ten illustrations from this volume may be reproduced on any one project or in any single publication, free and without special permission. Wherever possible a credit line should be included indicating title, author and publisher. Please address the publisher for permission to make more extensive use of illustrations than that authorized above. The reproduction of this book in whole is prohibited.

International Standard Book Number: 0-486-22740-5
Library of Congress Catalog Card Number: 78-151422

Manufactured in the United States of America
Dover Publications, Inc.
180 Varick Street
New York, N. Y. 10014

Publisher's Note

These one hundred and one drawings, in which social commentary is cast in the form of the ghoulish burlesque, represent the cream of Jan Faust's work to date. In a bold pen technique akin to that of Reginald Marsh, Mr. Faust is working today in the time-honored tradition of such older masters as Gillray, Goya, Daumier, Grandville, Kley and Grosz. In their arresting and compelling visions, barbed as they are with macabre or whimsical humor, these artists have always touched the sore spots of society and recorded the secret anxieties of their age more surely and poisonously than the grandiose or intellectualized works of their contemporaries.

It is a strange world, this of Mr. Faust's, but it is unmistakably ours. In these days of supermachines, antimatter and multidimensionality, is it any wonder that his animate beings turn into mechanisms, while his manufactured gadgets sprout living parts? Or that his creatures undergo a constant uneasy shifting between man and animal, between person and garment? What is more representative of our age than these false fronts and deceptive façades, this irruption of the unexpected and unnerving into such hallowed domains of rationality and smugness as the breakfast table and the nursery, where odd transformations beset the doll, the teddy bear and Daisy Duck? The note of protest could hardly be absent from a collection like this, but the antimilitary and antipollution outcries included here are themselves tinged with this artist's particular madness.

Surely Mr. Faust's overriding preoccupation, as he examines our sex-obsessed society, is with the flesh—erogenous, erupting, melting, de- and recomposing. We find eerily wandering anatomical parts (like Shelley's vision of eyes in women's breasts); a serpent burrowing through a ravaged face (strongly reminiscent of Gillray's gout demon); a proliferation of genitals and mammaries; intercourse in the shadow of the tomb.

Yet these are not grim or depressing pictures. This namesake and modern avatar of the medieval alchemist Johannes Faustus transmutes all he touches into fantasy and humor. His work abounds in visual puns—the "menace of television," the man "supporting his family"—and in fanciful answers to whimsical questions: What would a dog look like in pants? What about an elephant on roller skates? The logic of the illogical exerts a strong fascination on his inquiring pen, and even the relatively few sheets containing straight reportage of the current scene are far from drily factual.

The underground of today may very well become the brightly lit, safe-for-everyone, thoroughfare of tomorrow. But the time for adventurous souls to explore its murky meanders is now, while the excitement of discovery and creation is still fresh. Mr. Faust is an eminently qualified guide.

The drawings

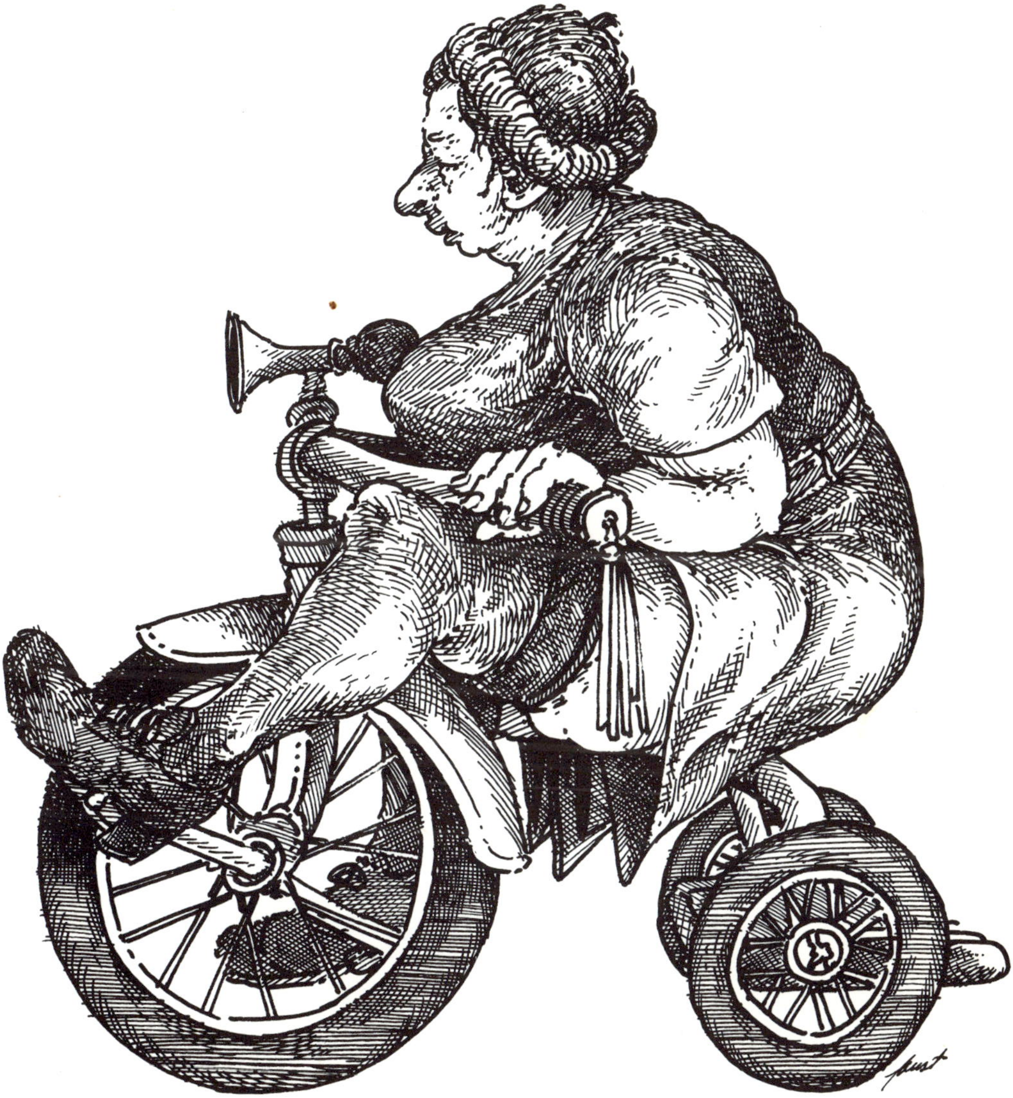

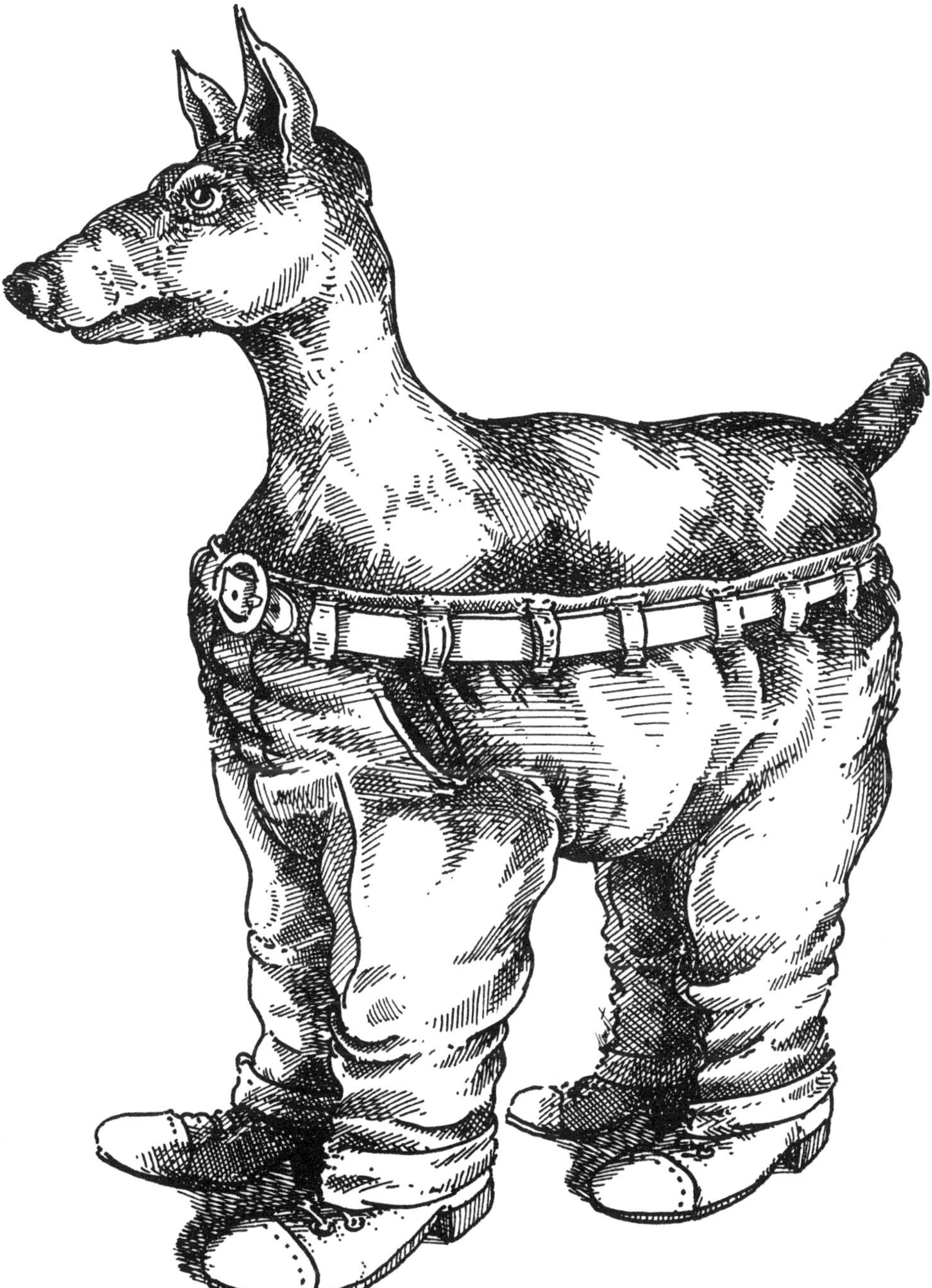

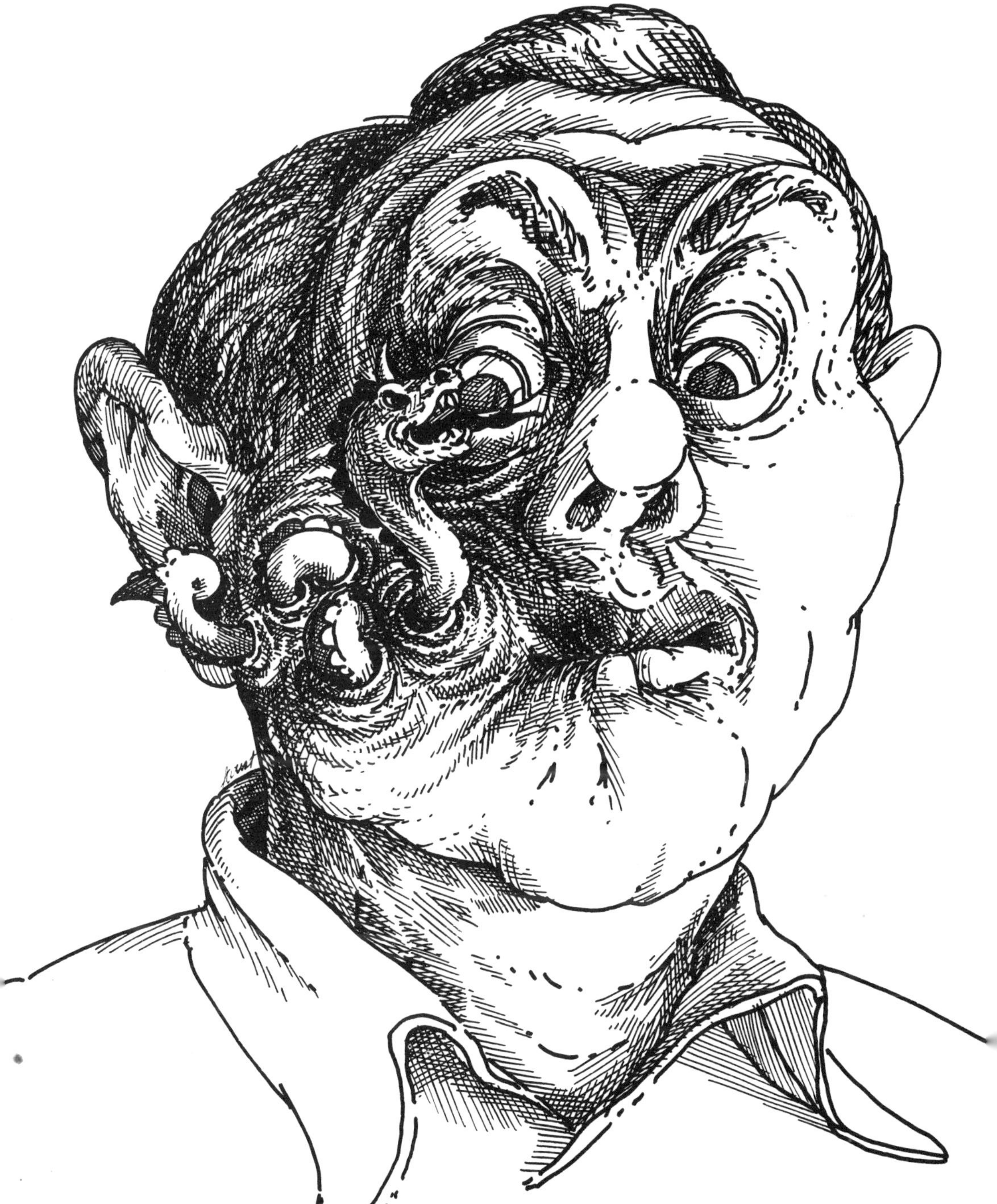

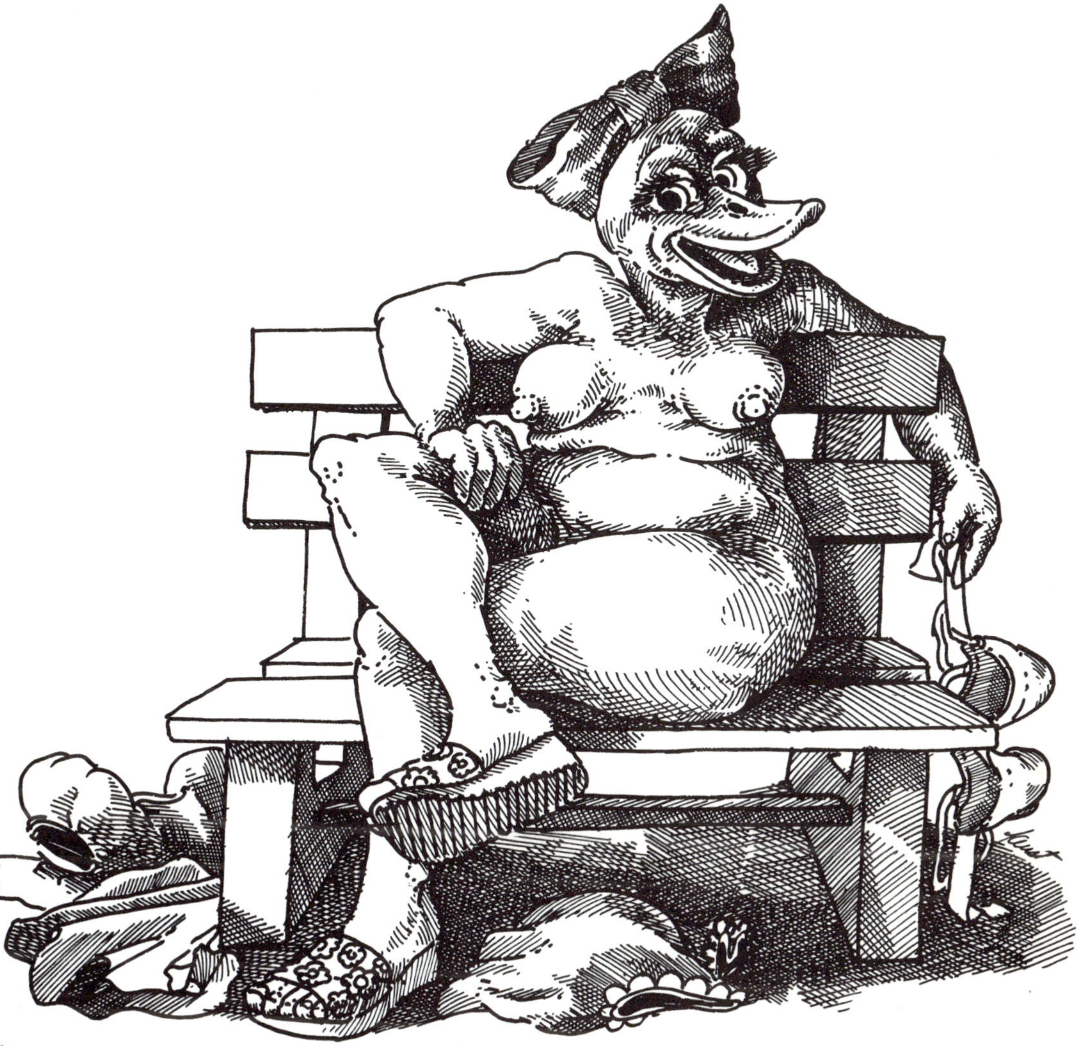

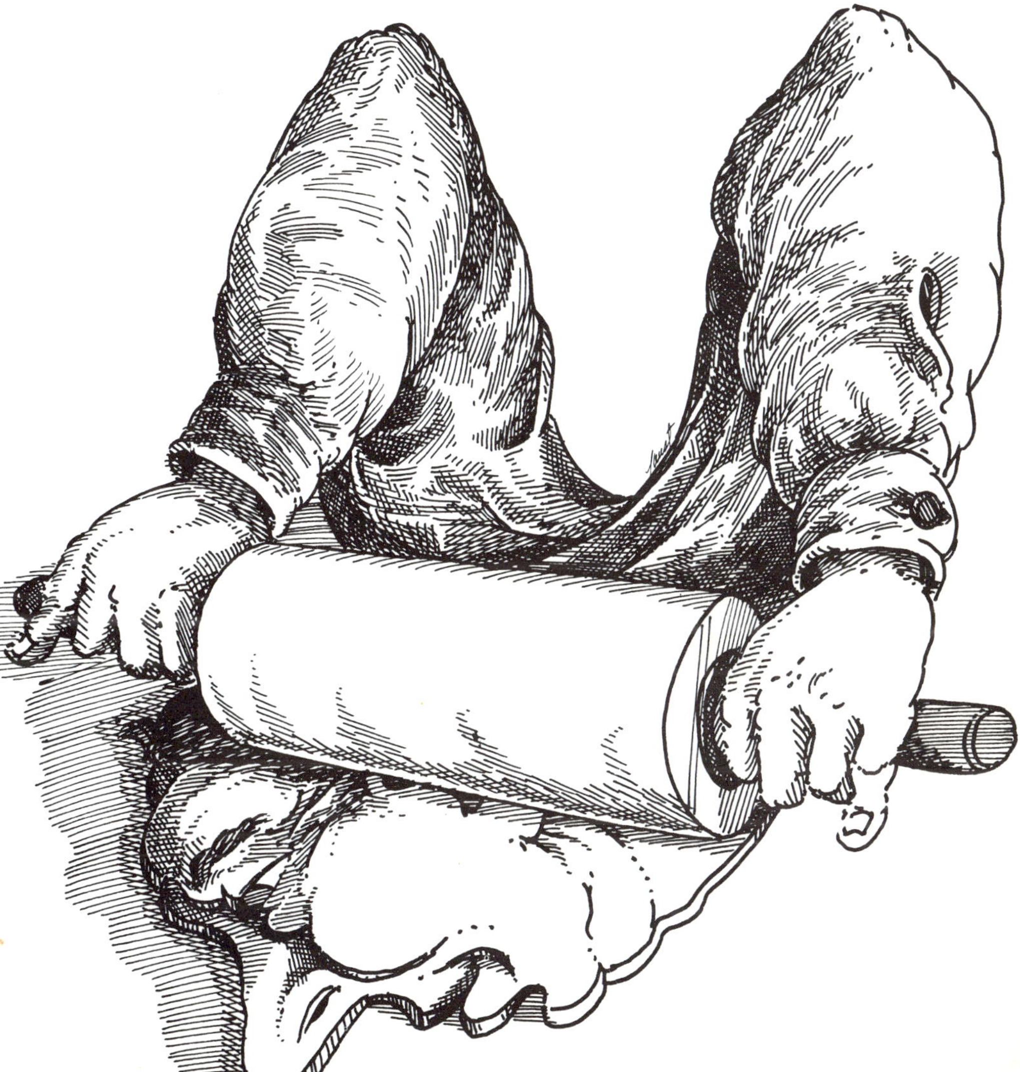

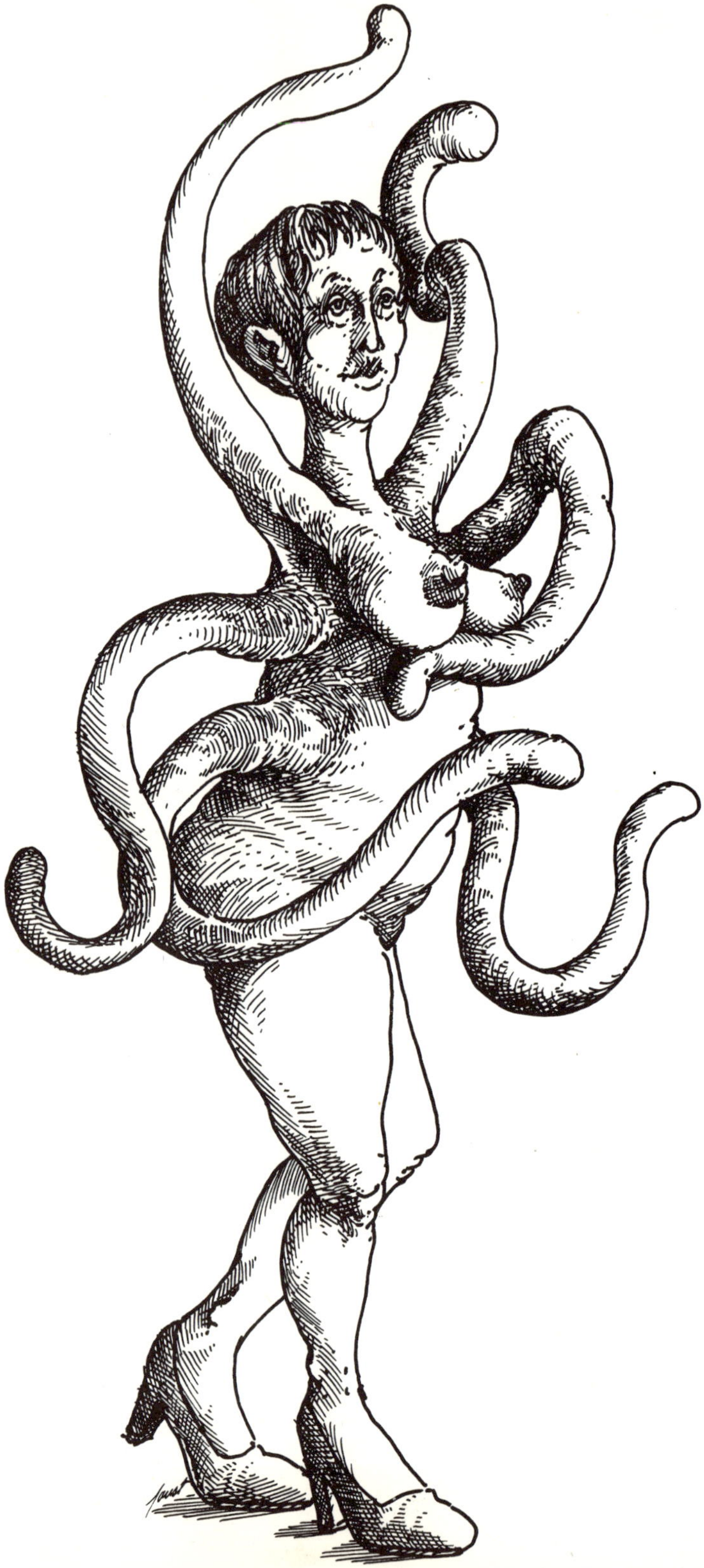

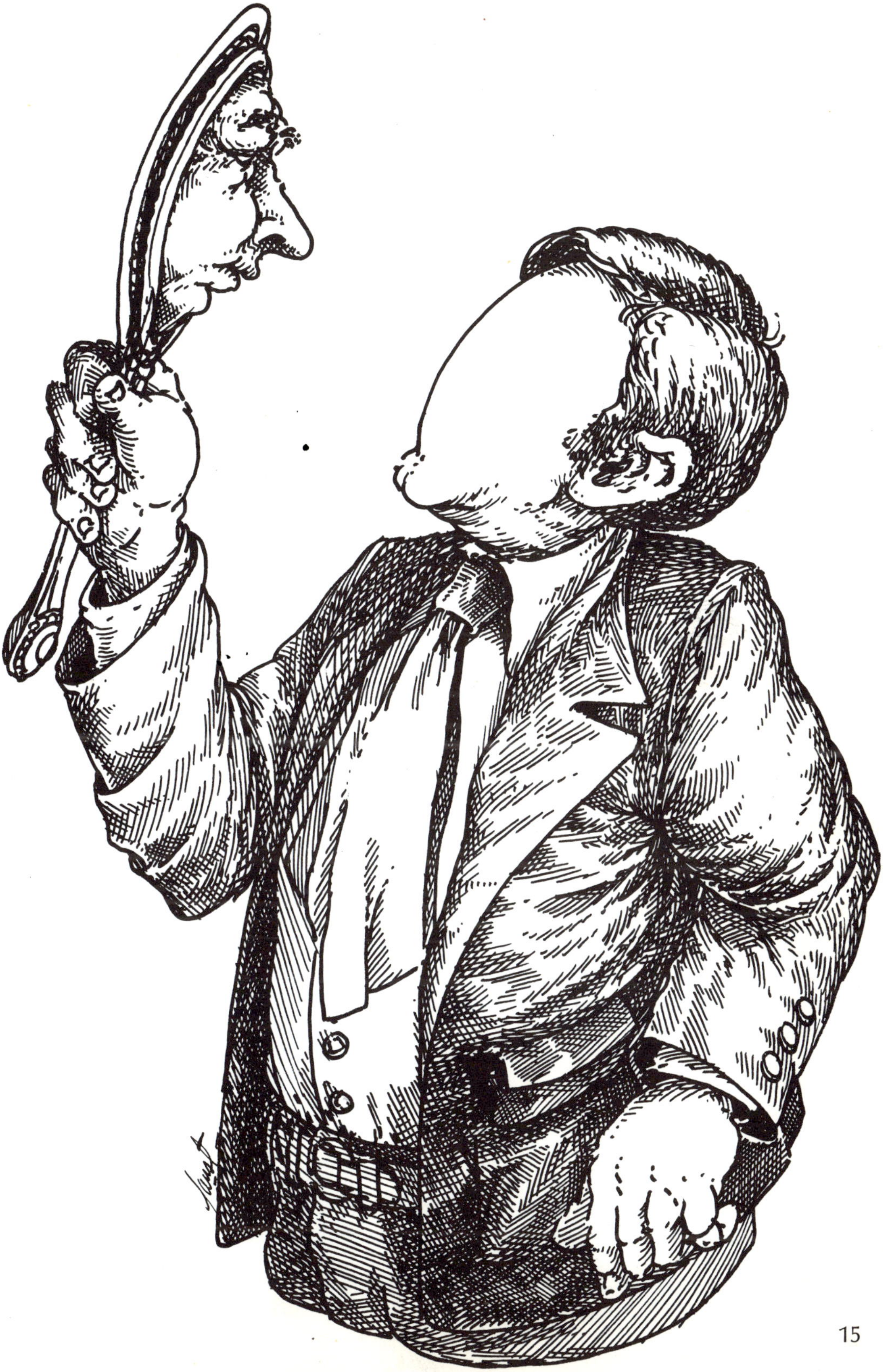

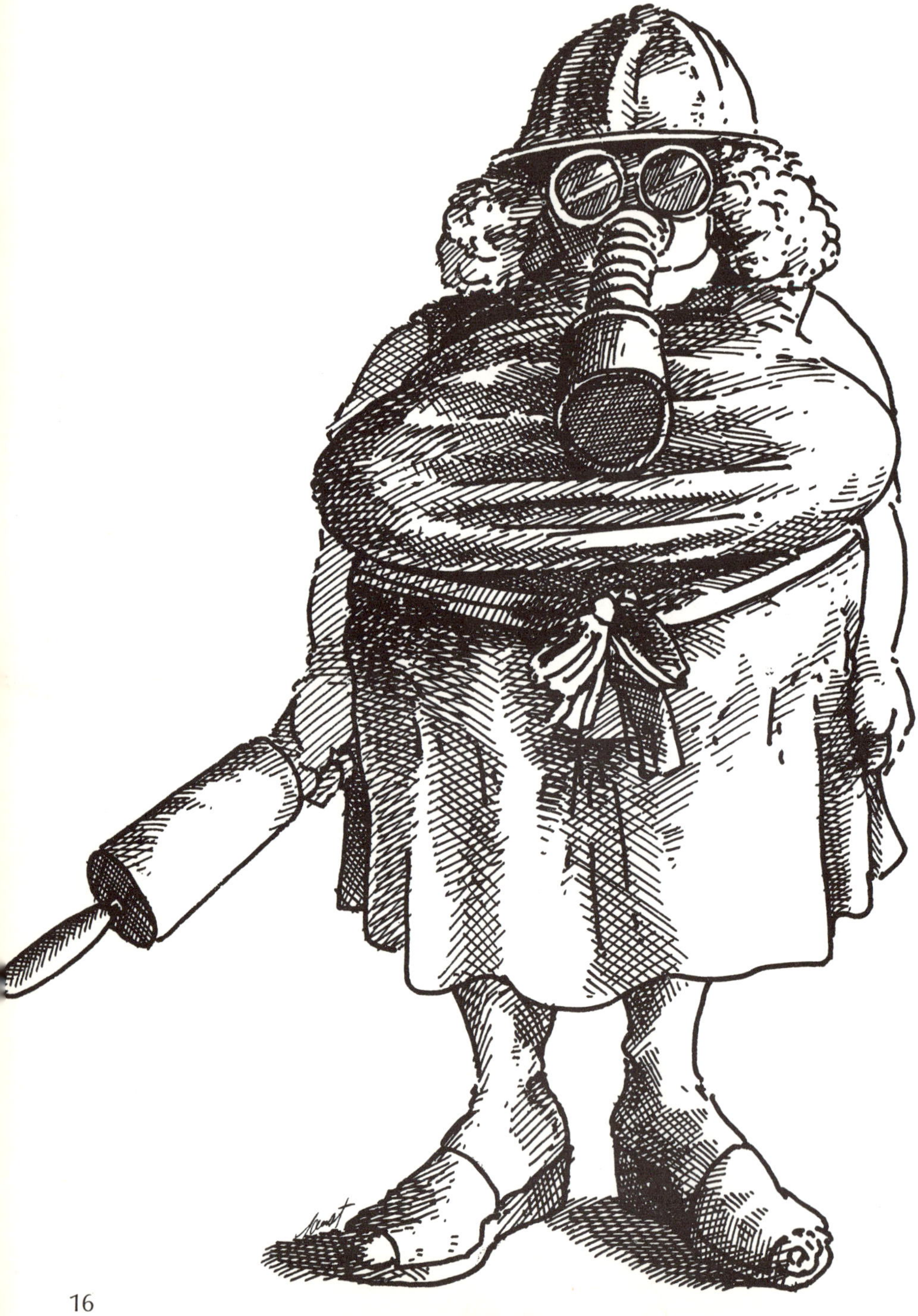

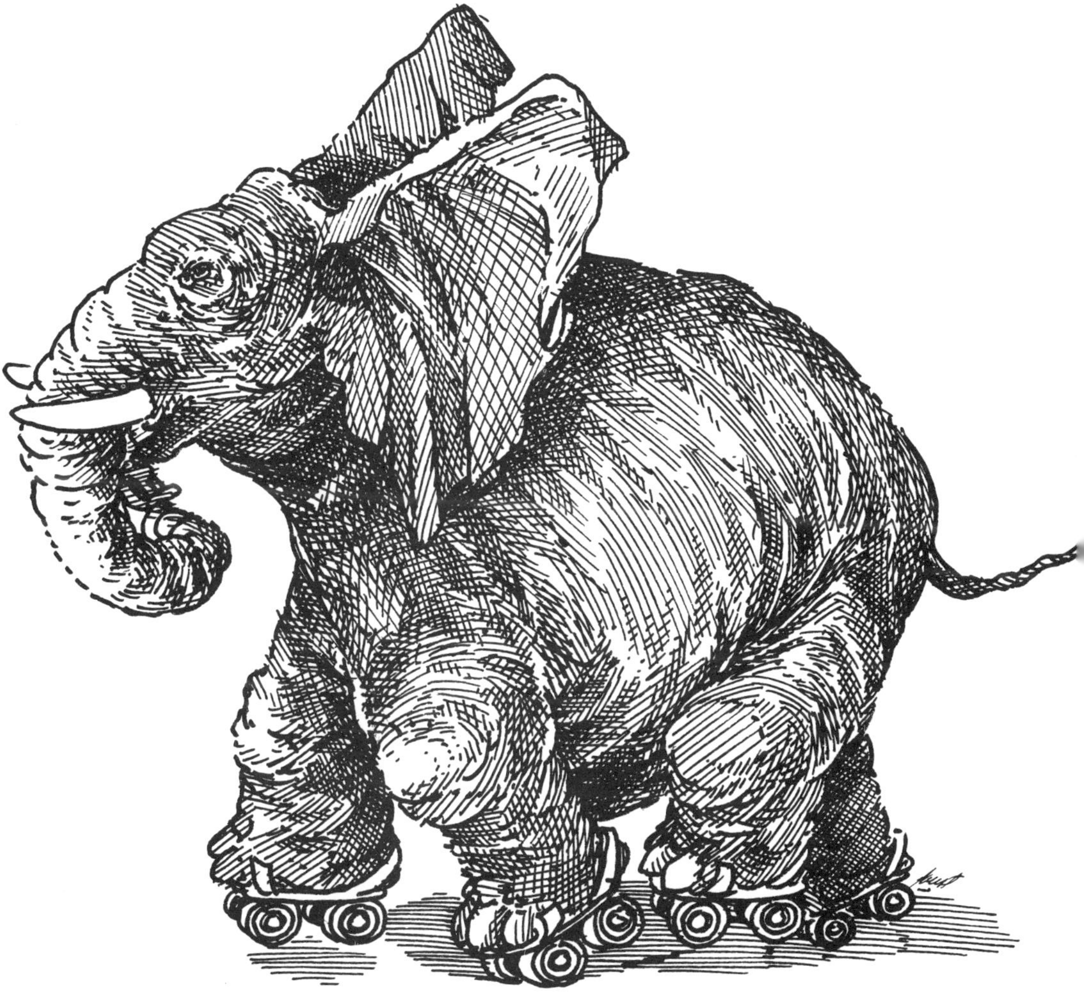

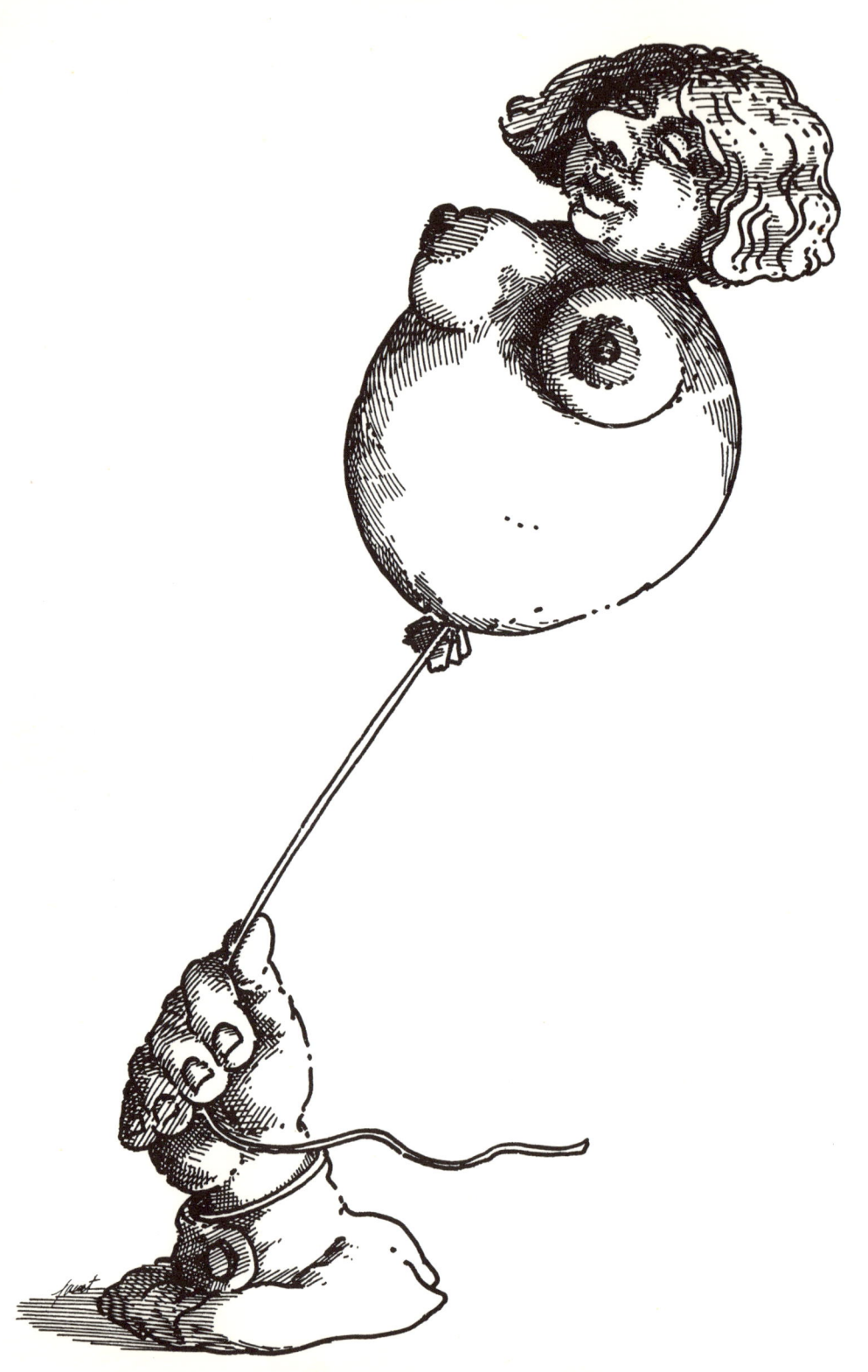

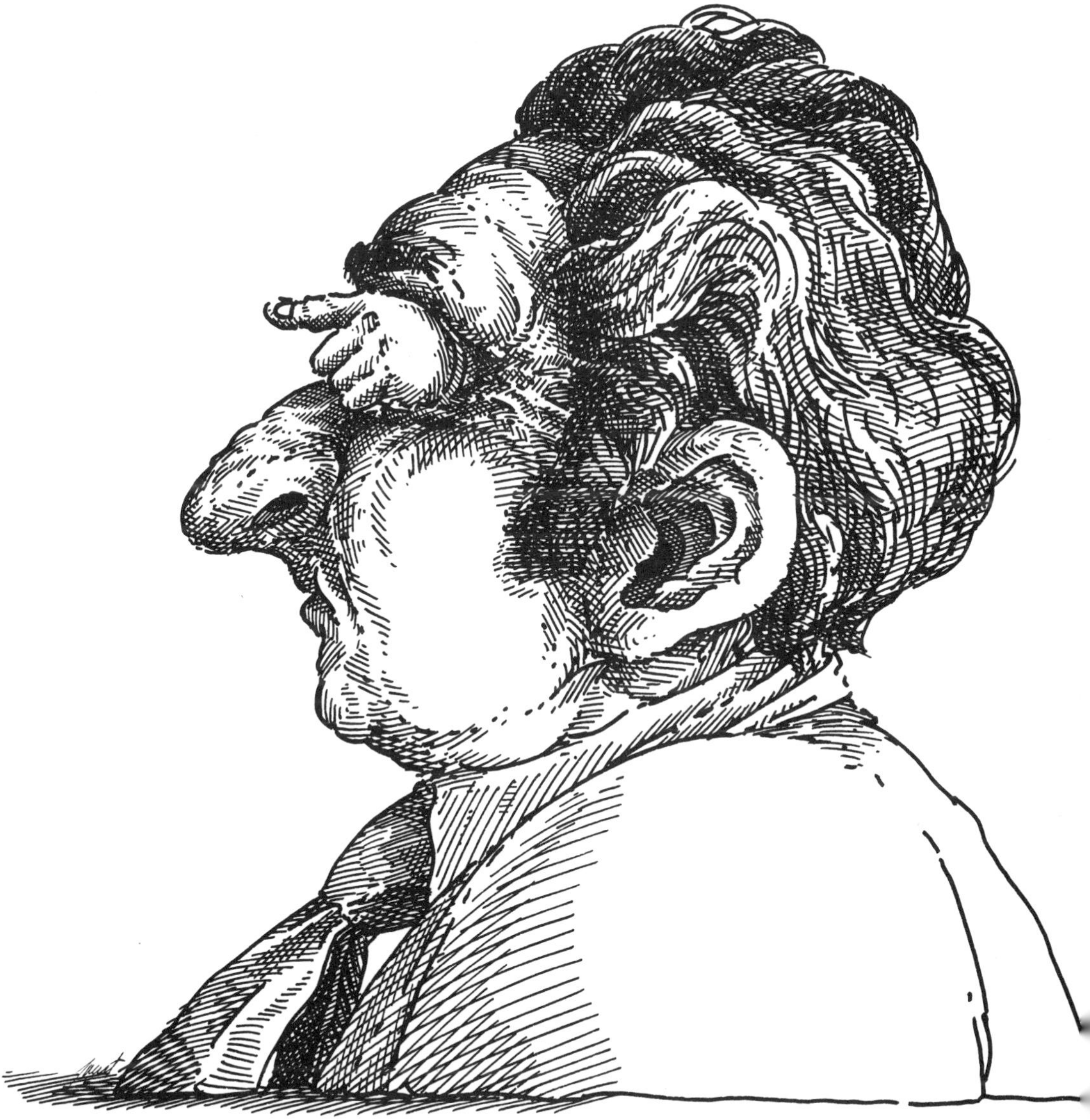

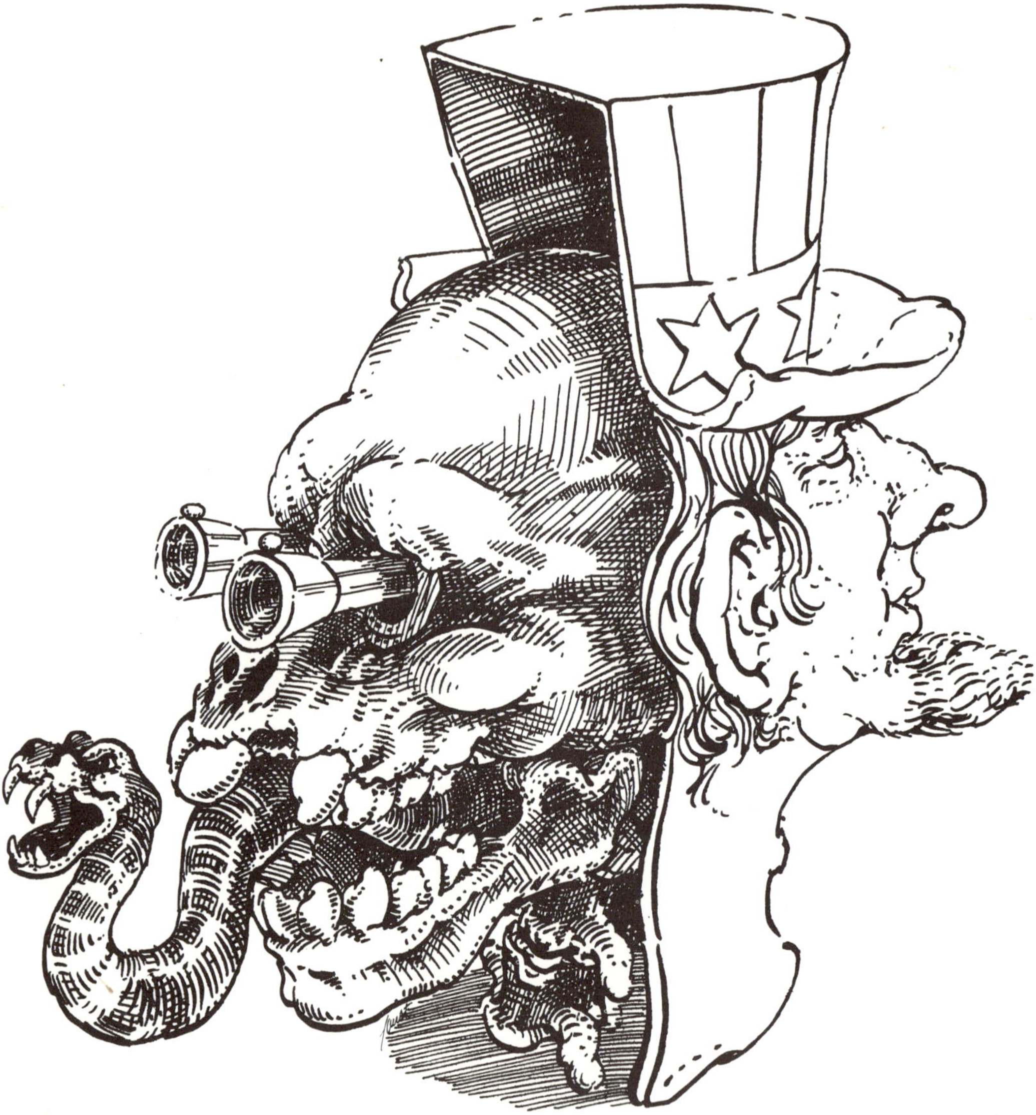

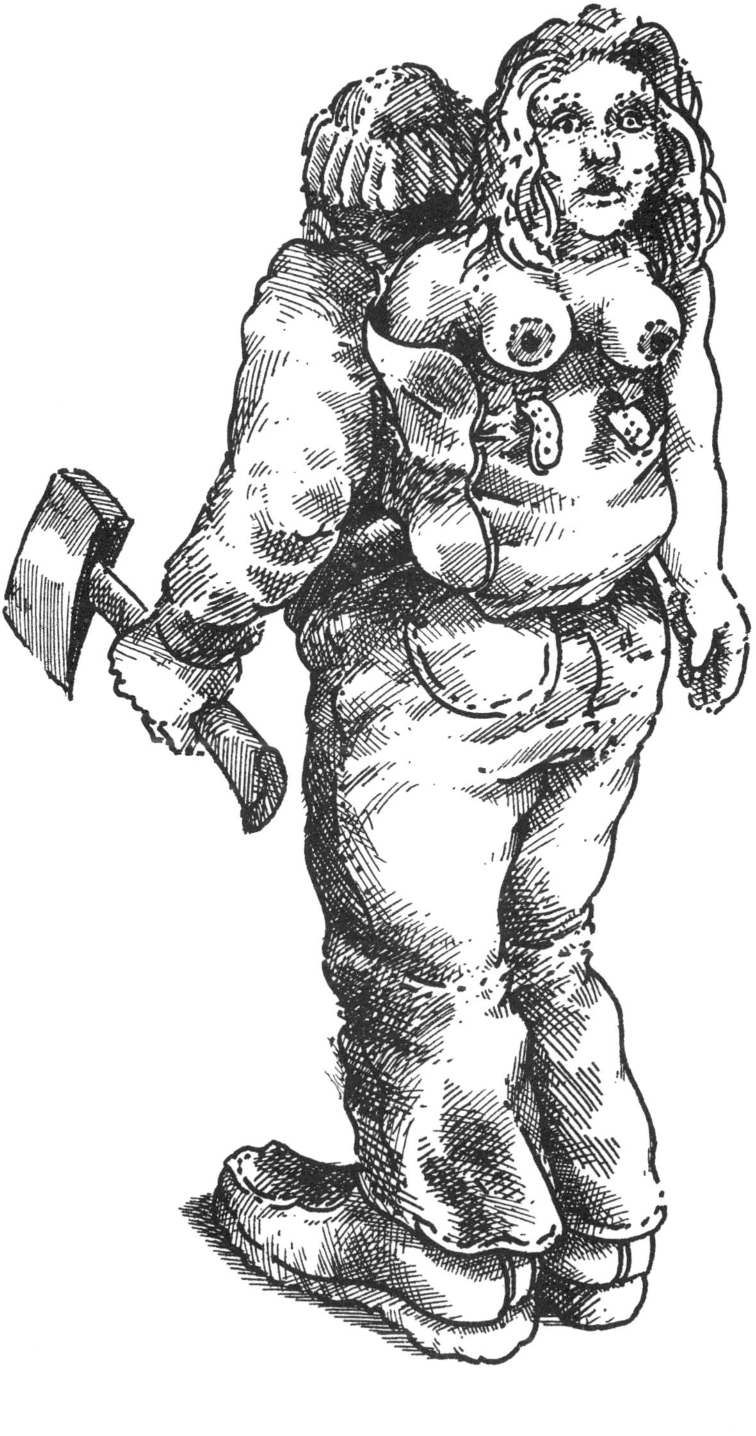

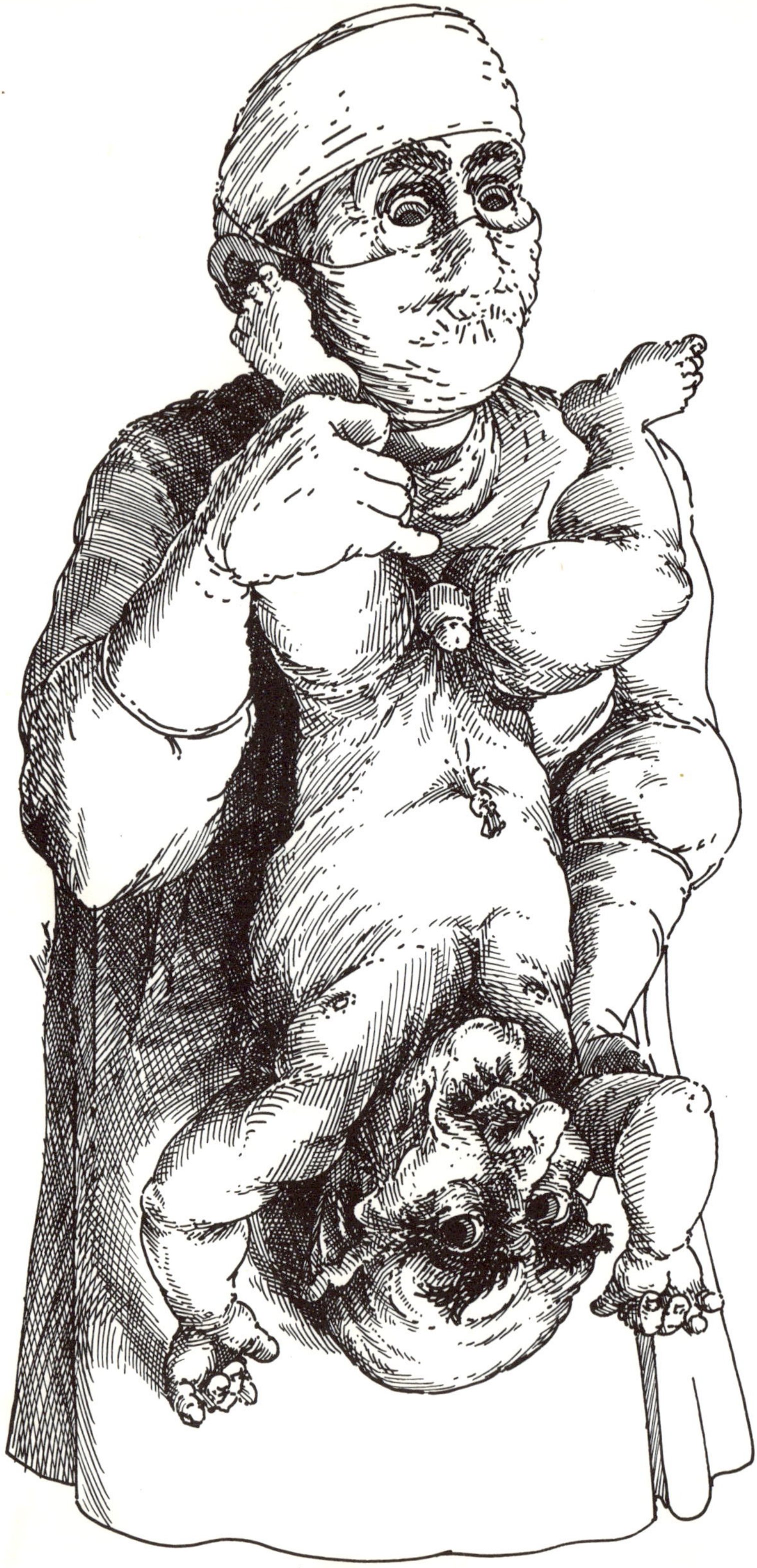

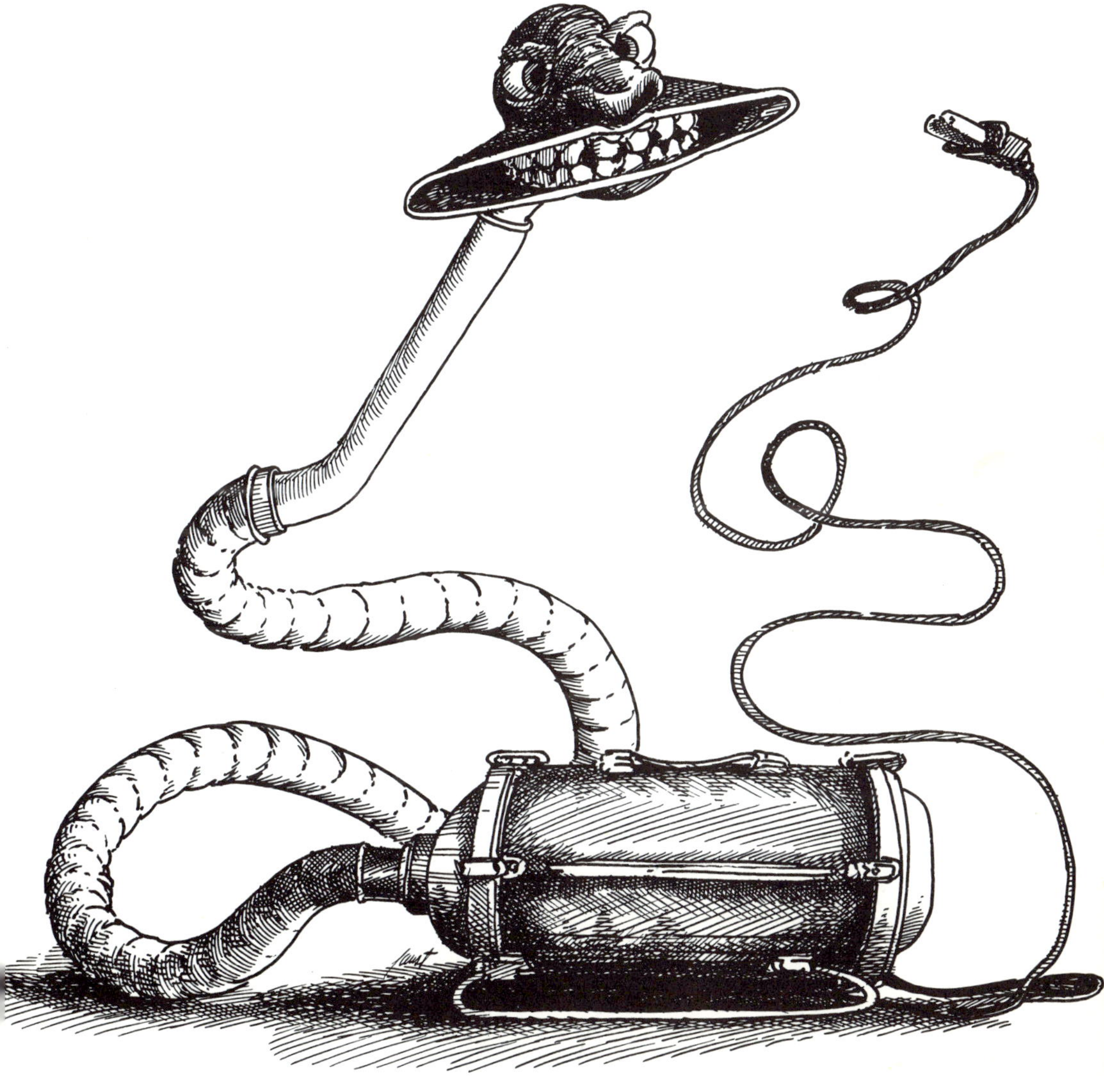

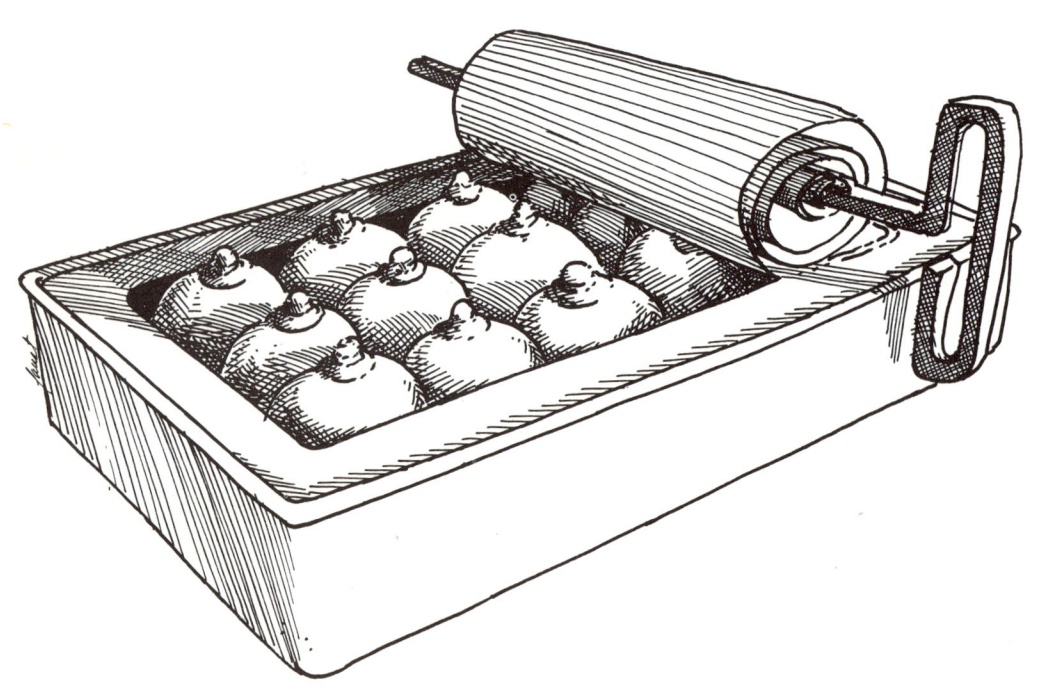

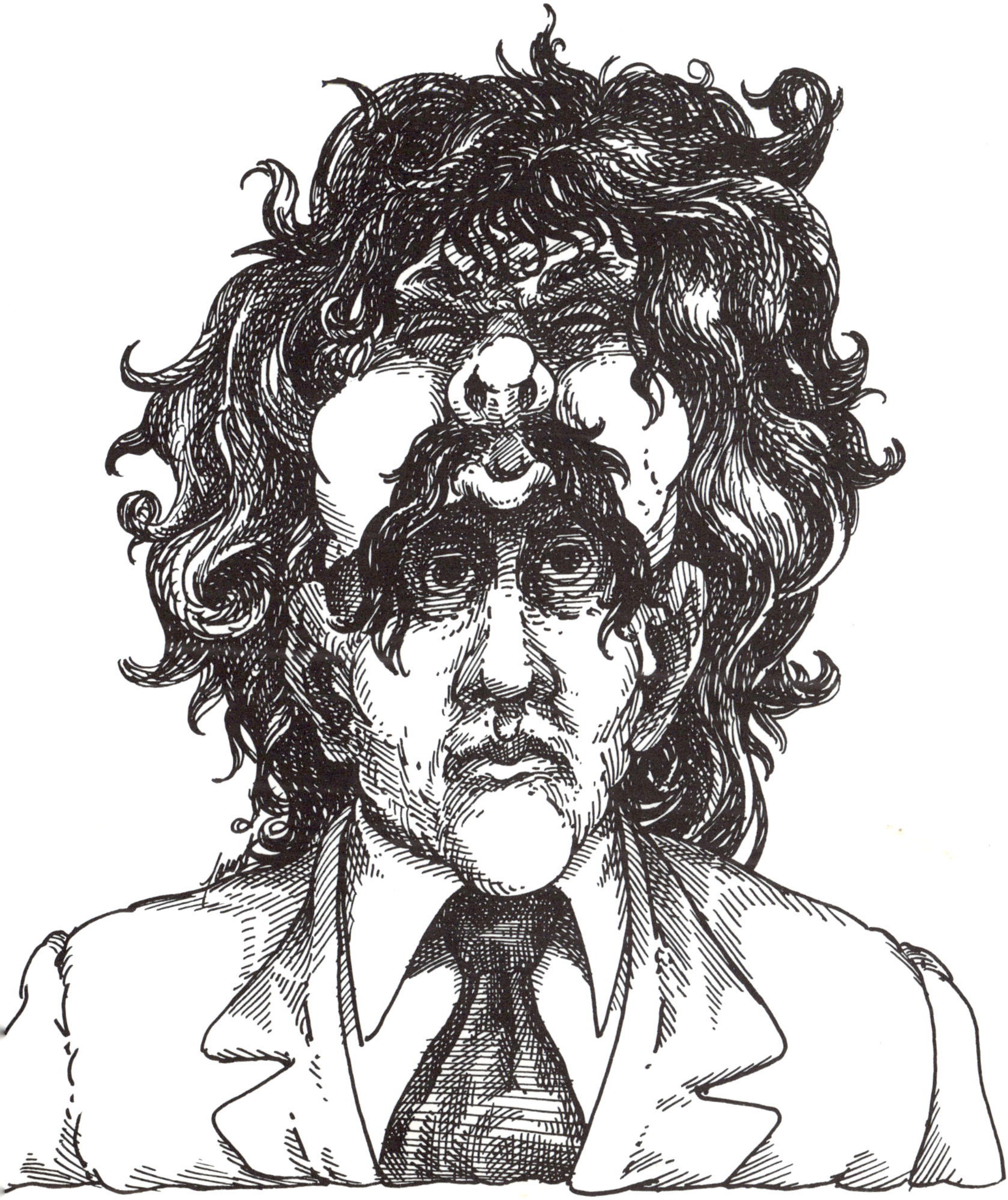

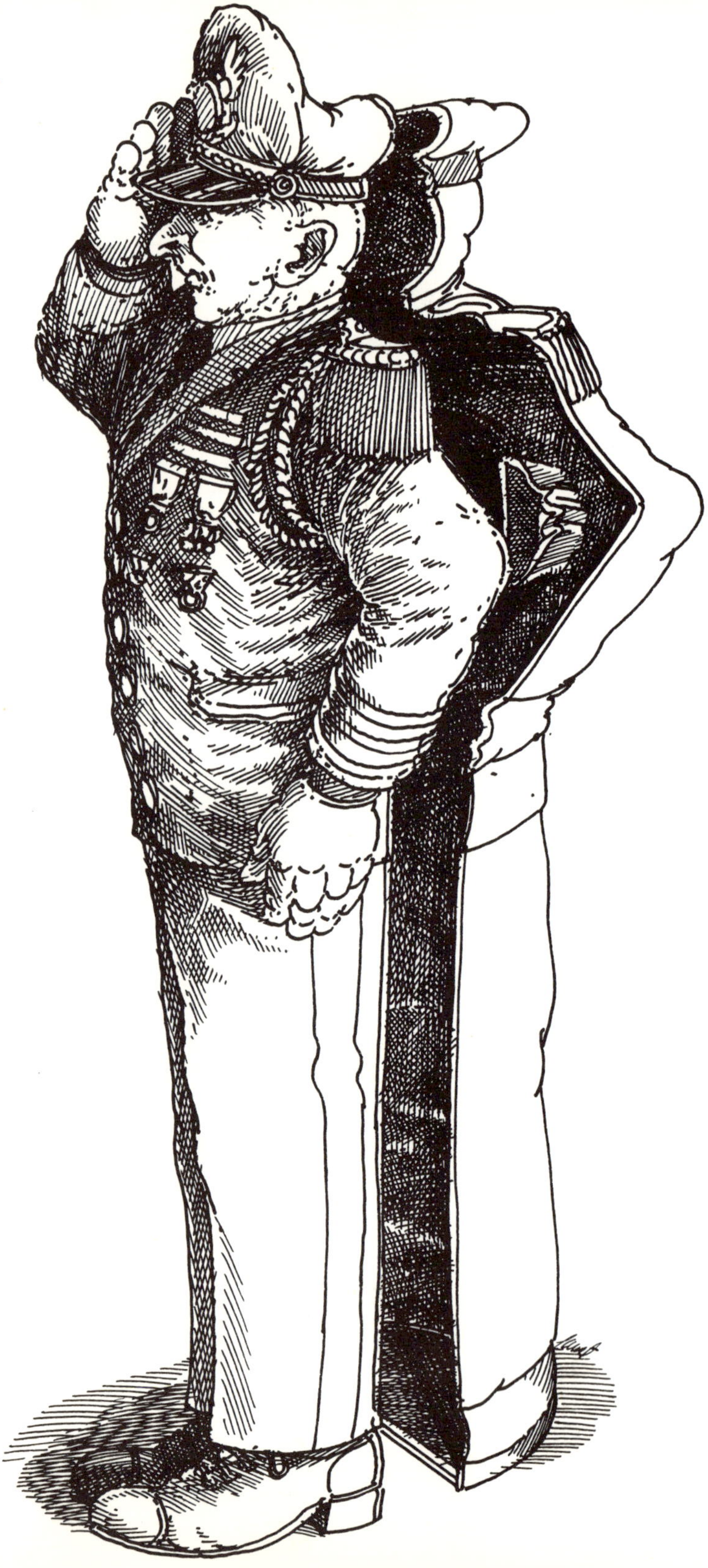

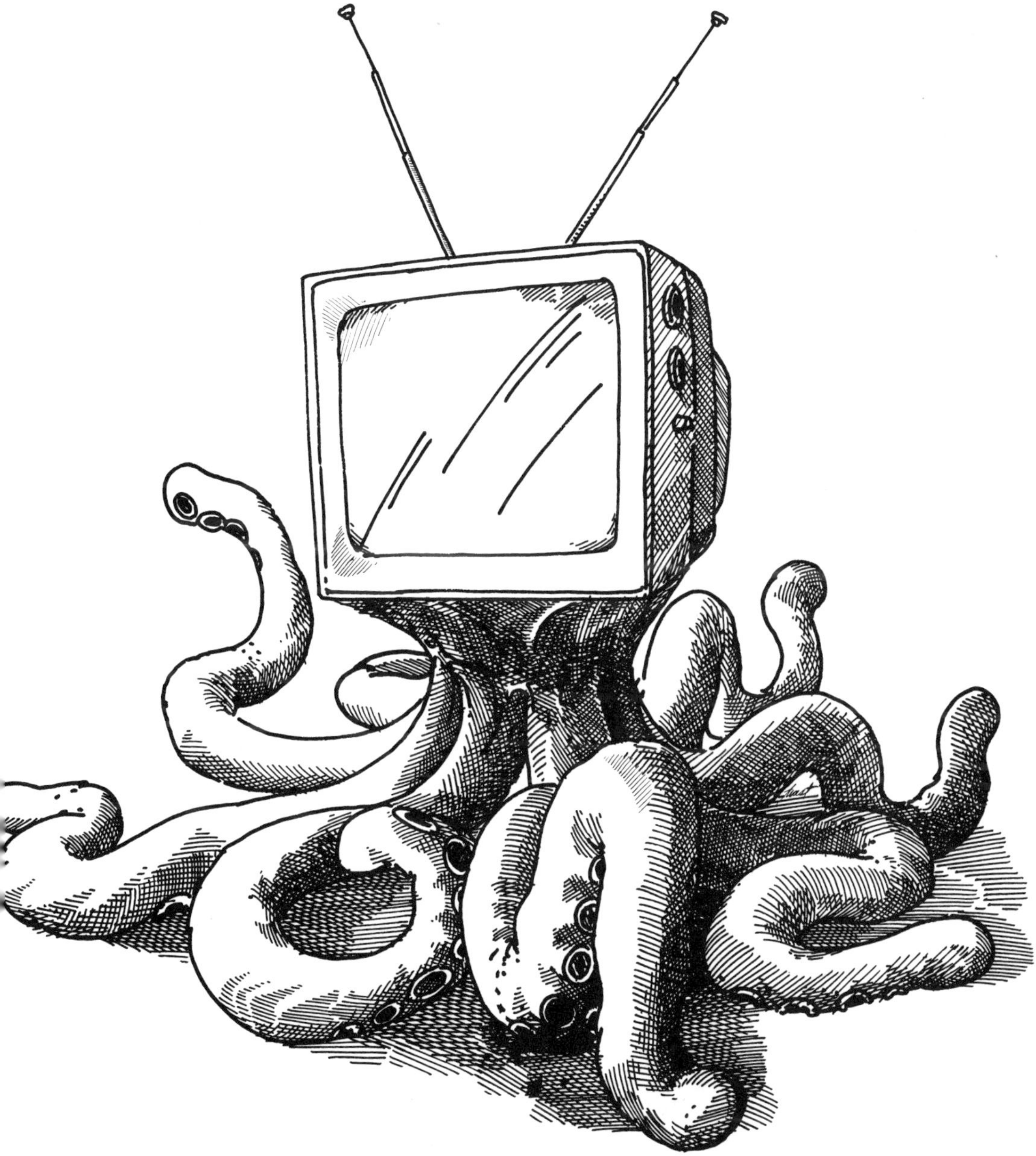

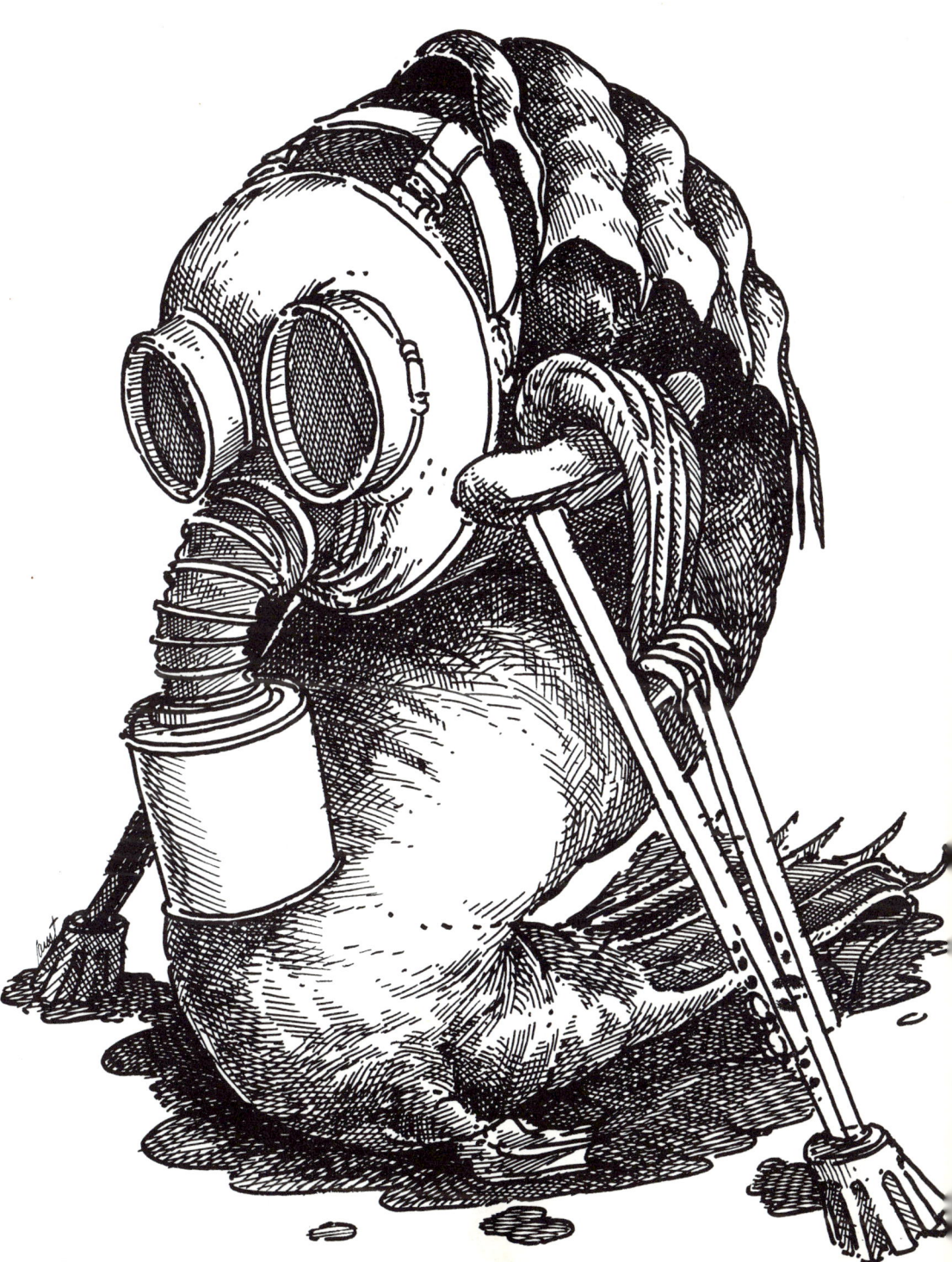

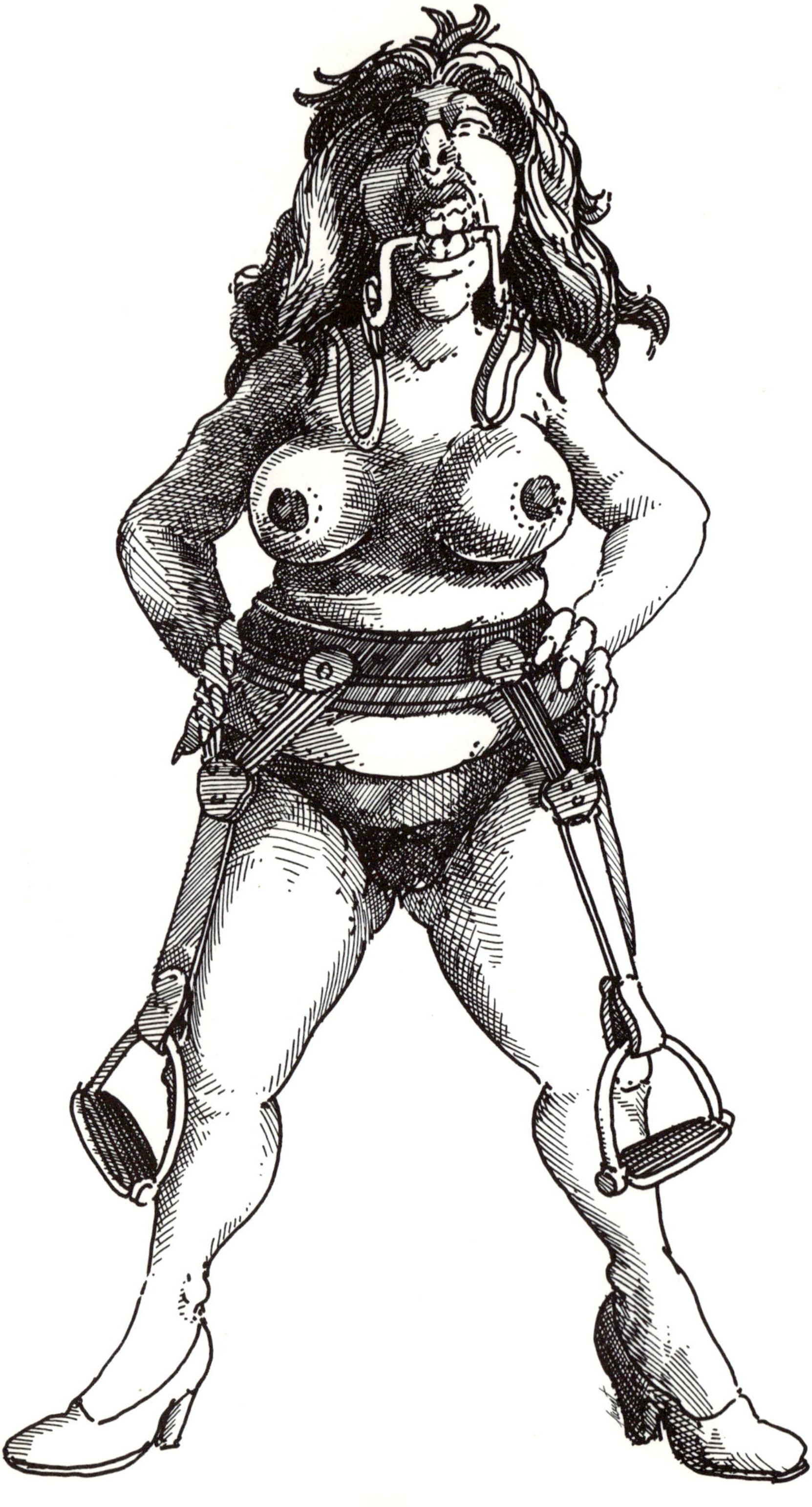

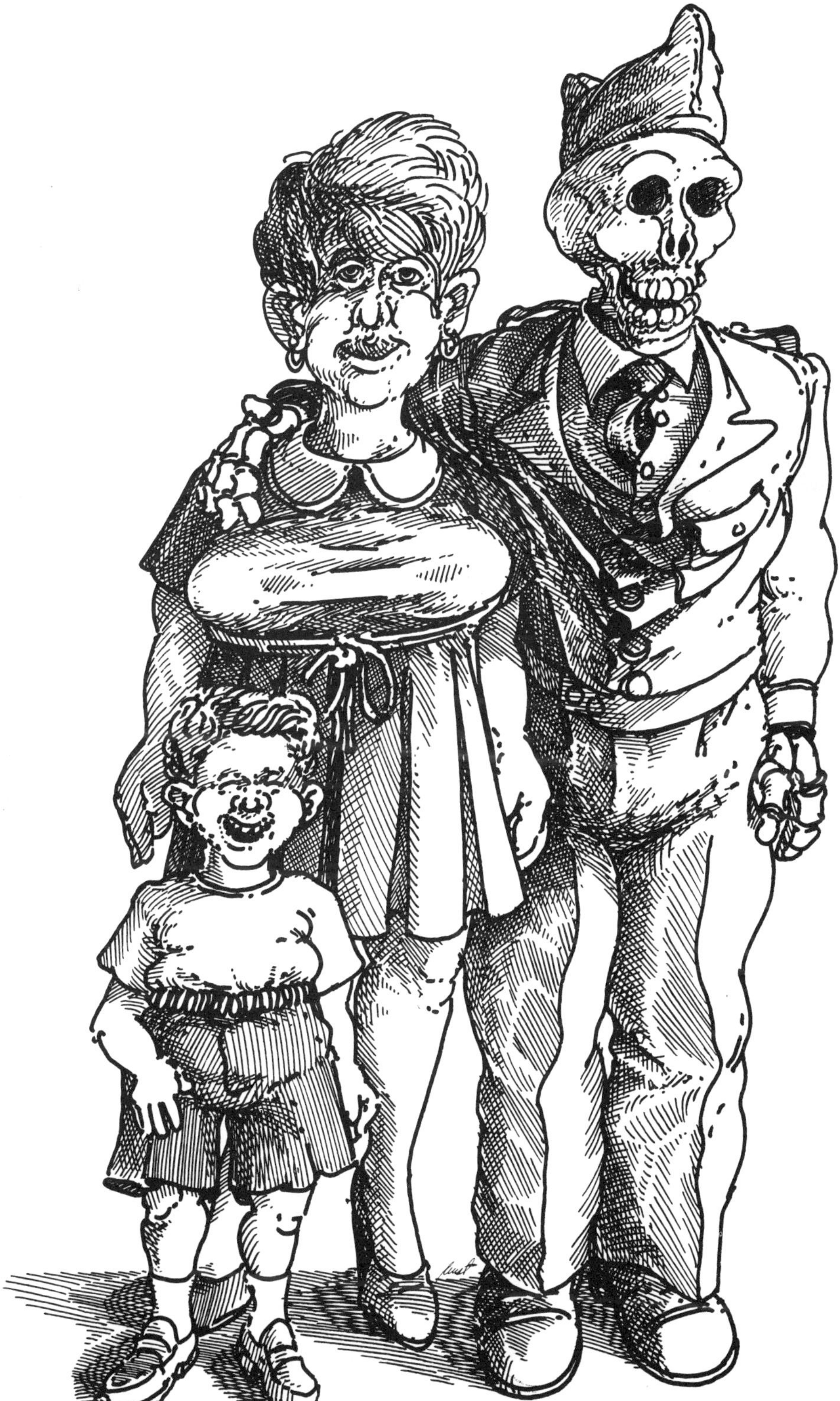

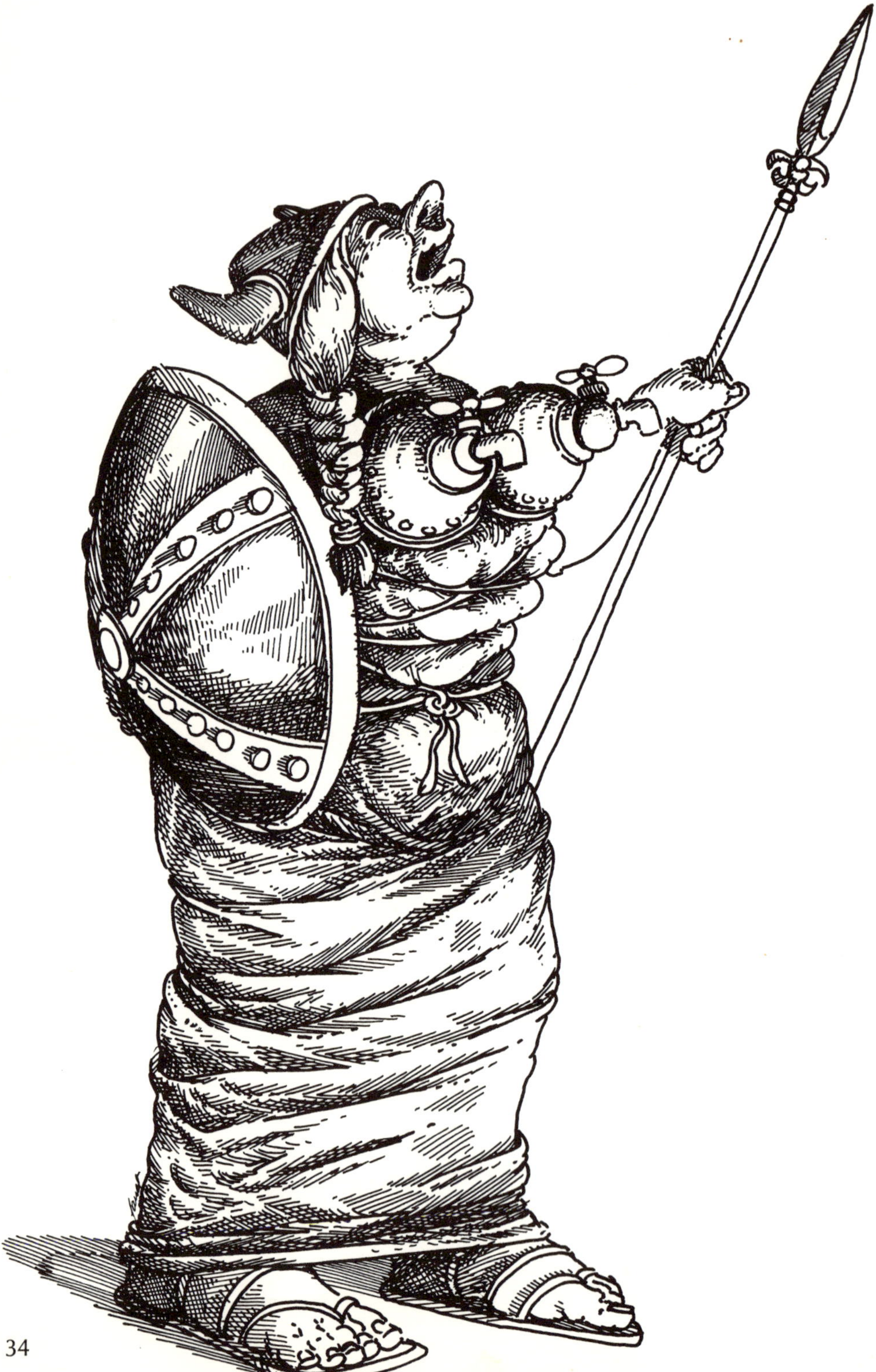

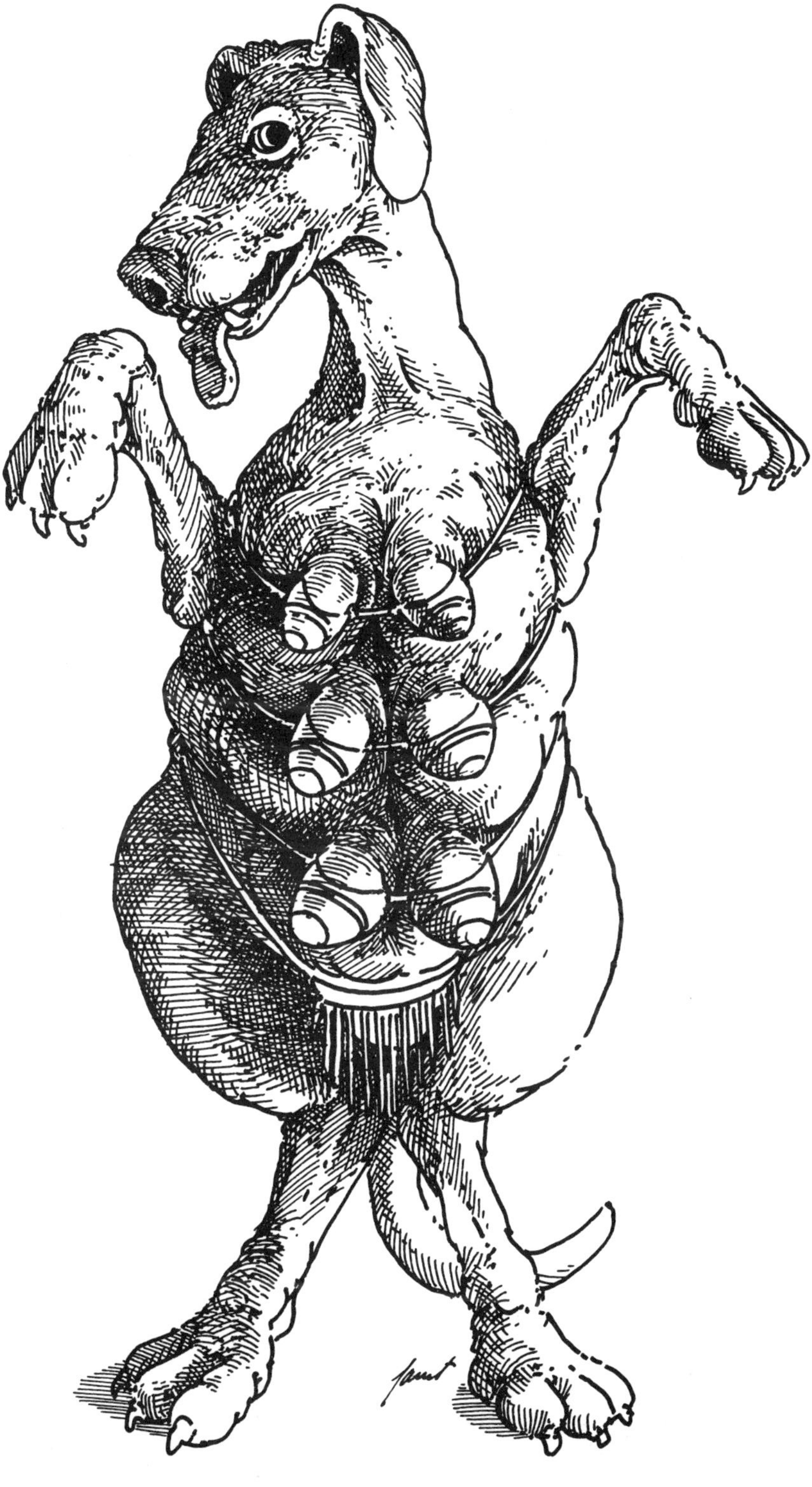

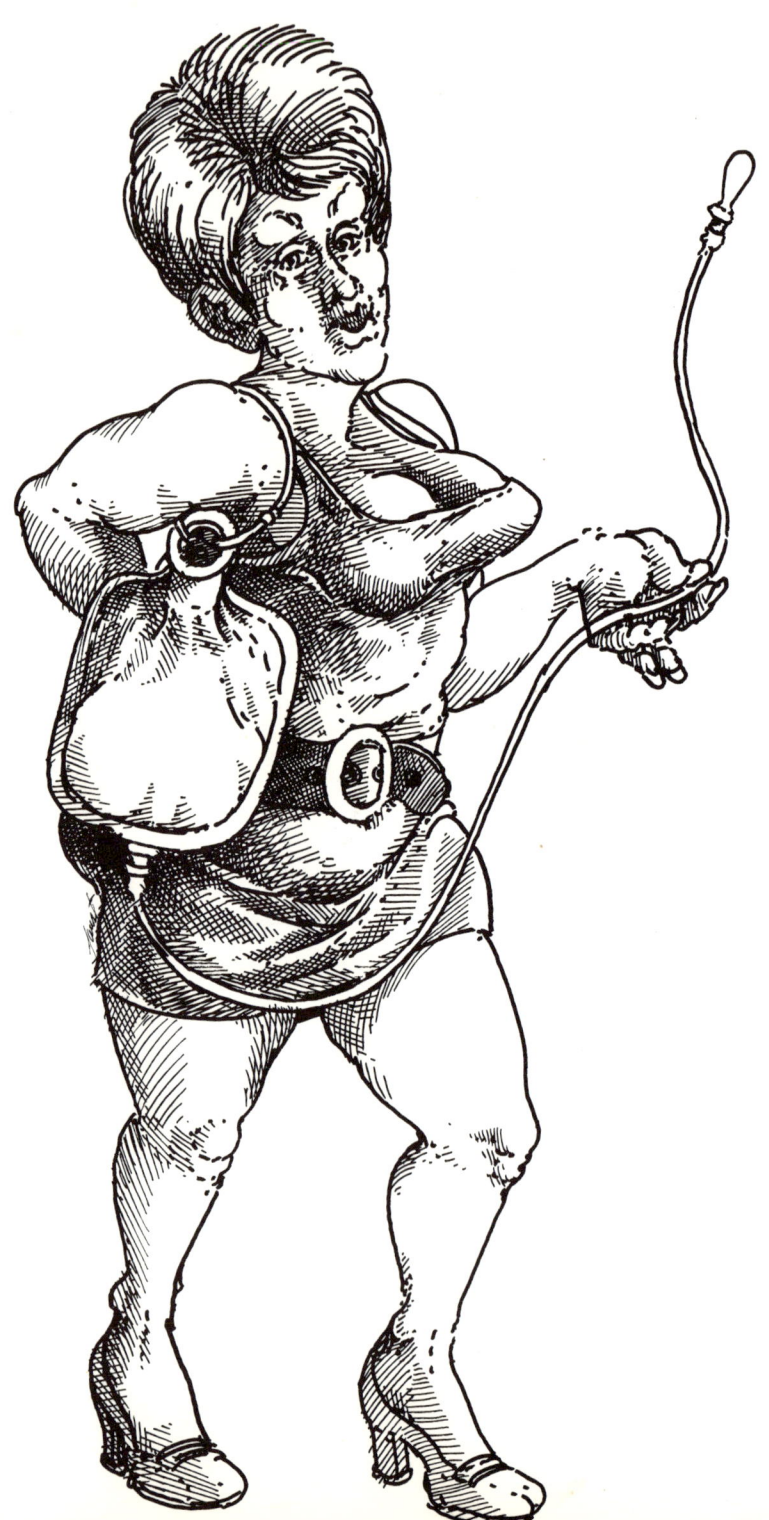

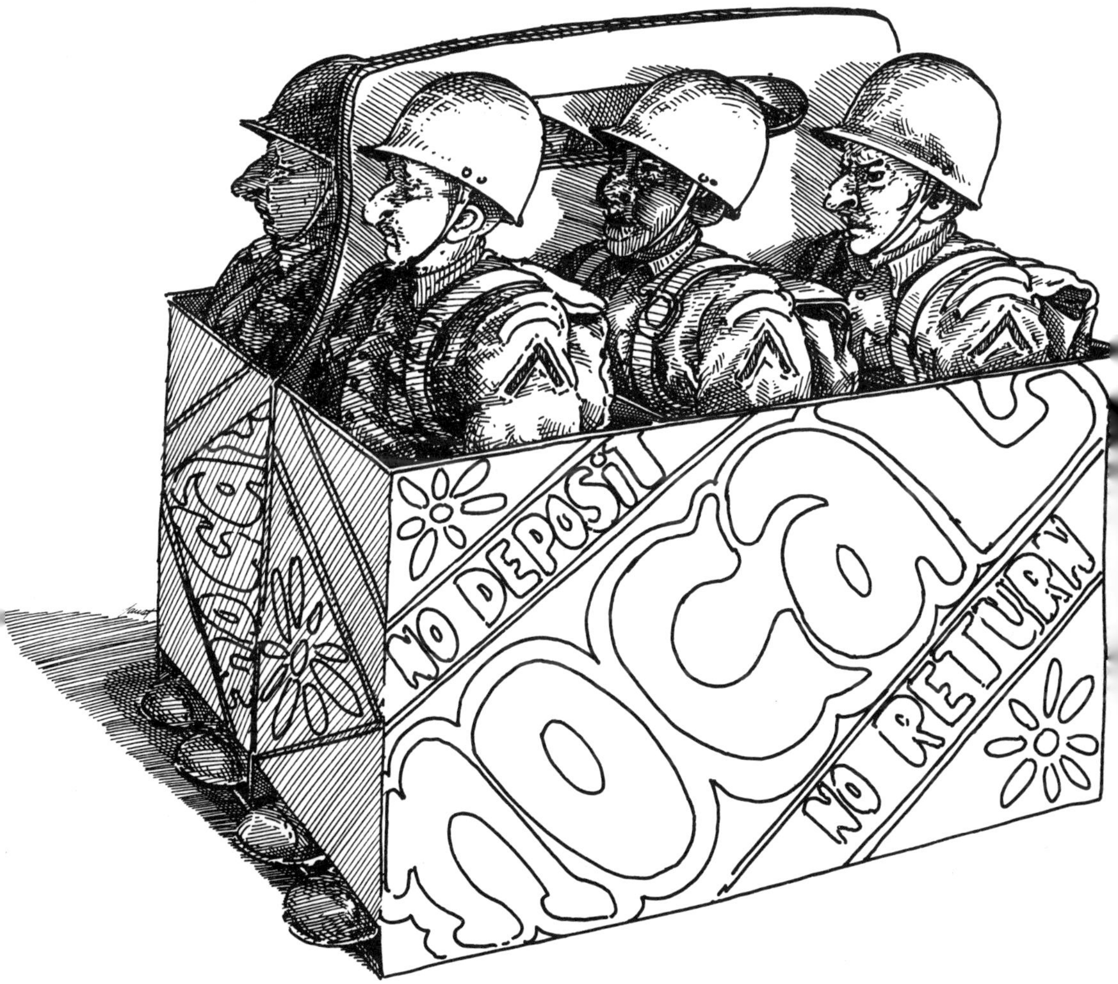
NO DEPOSIT
nocal
NO RETURN

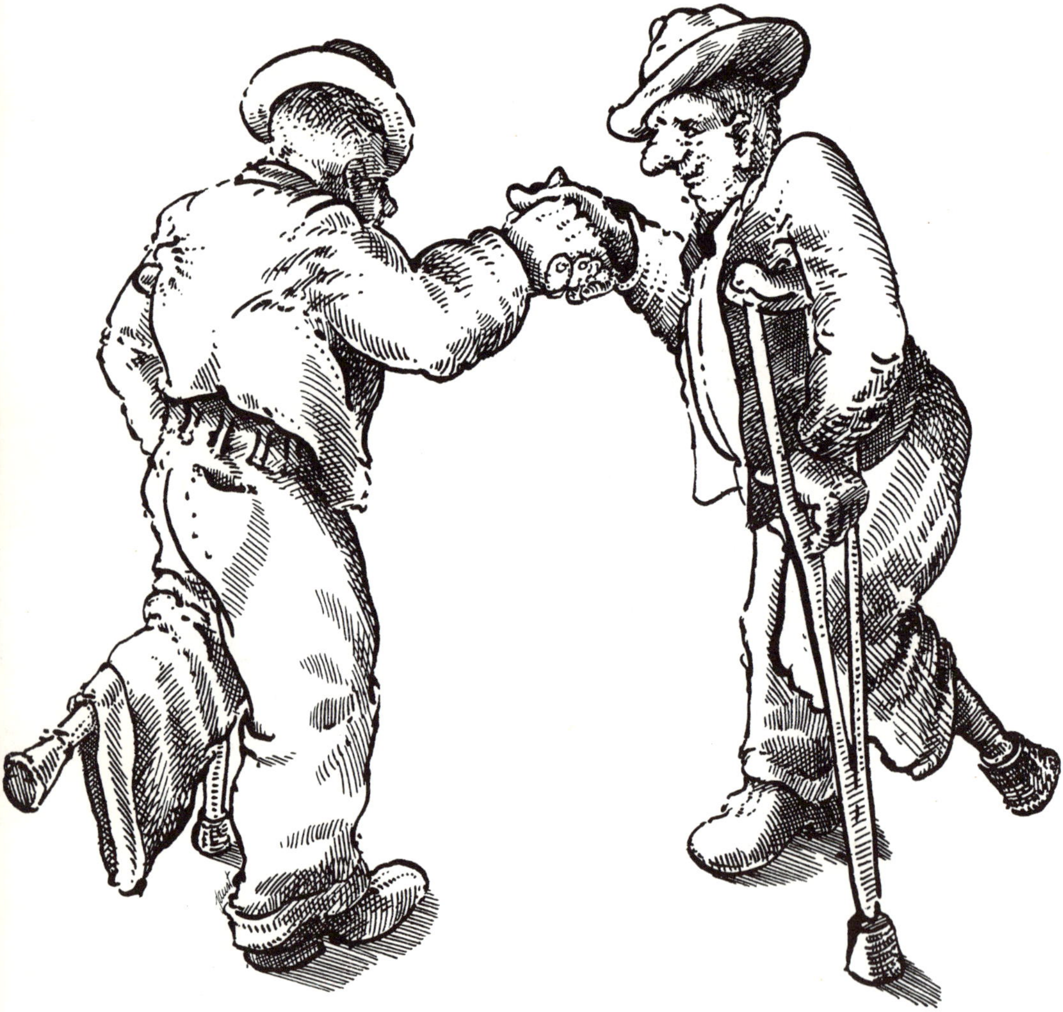

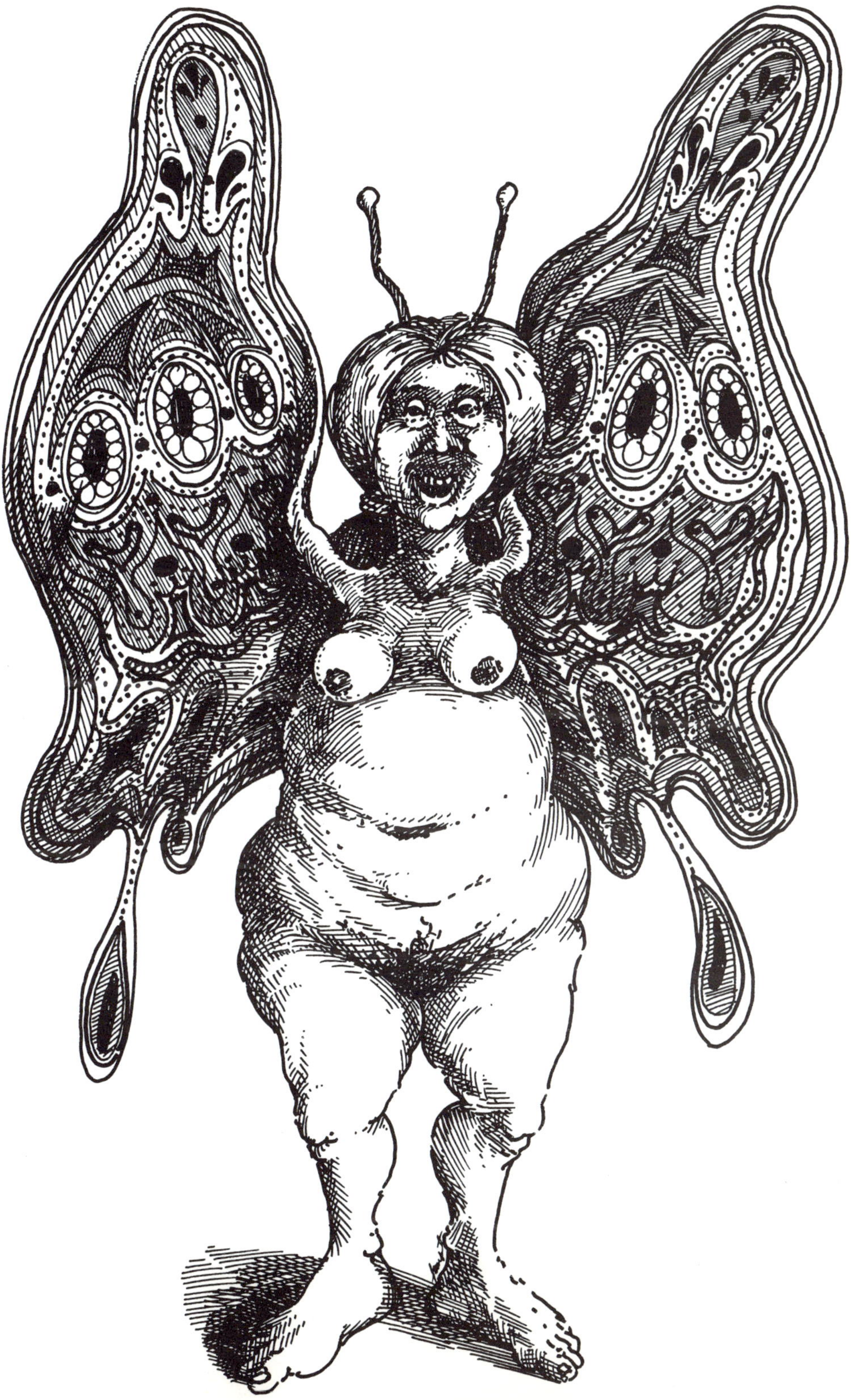

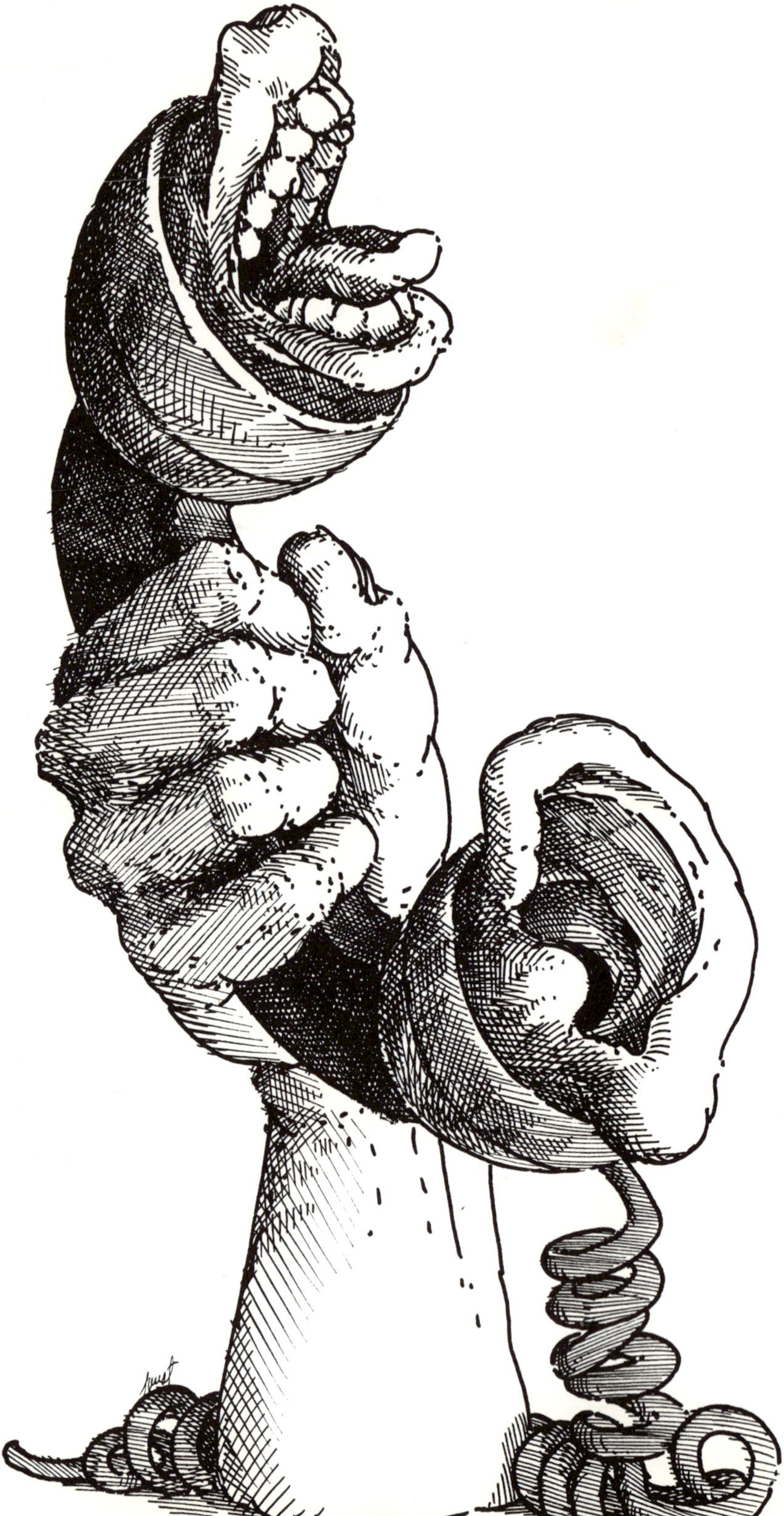

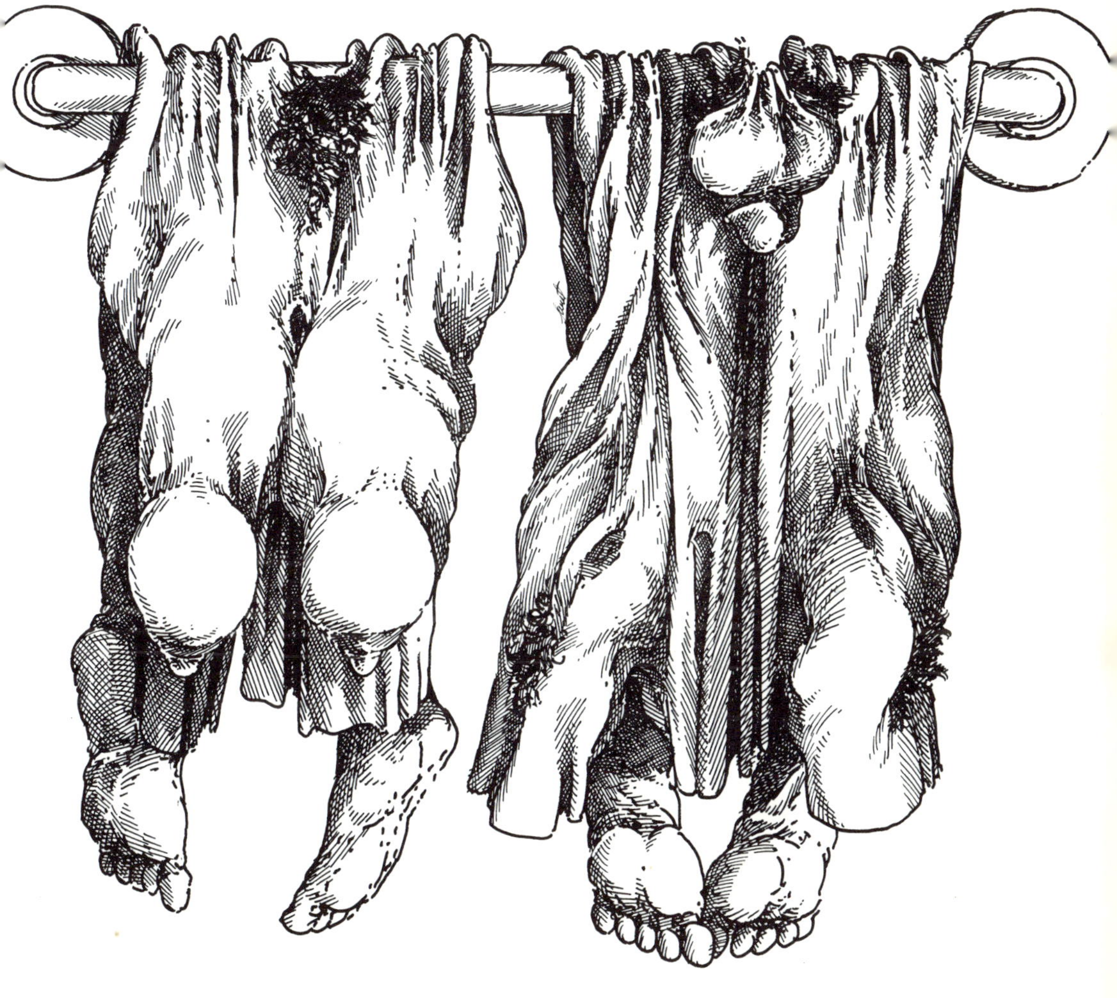

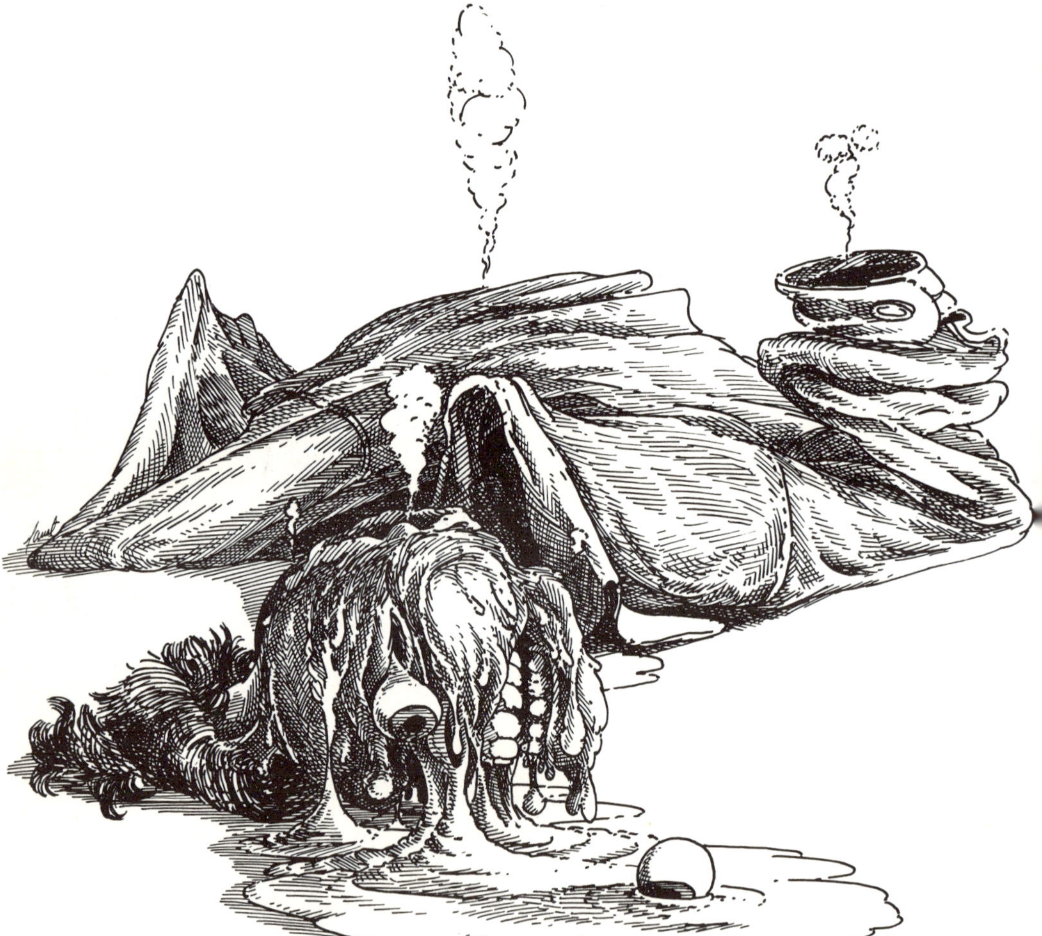

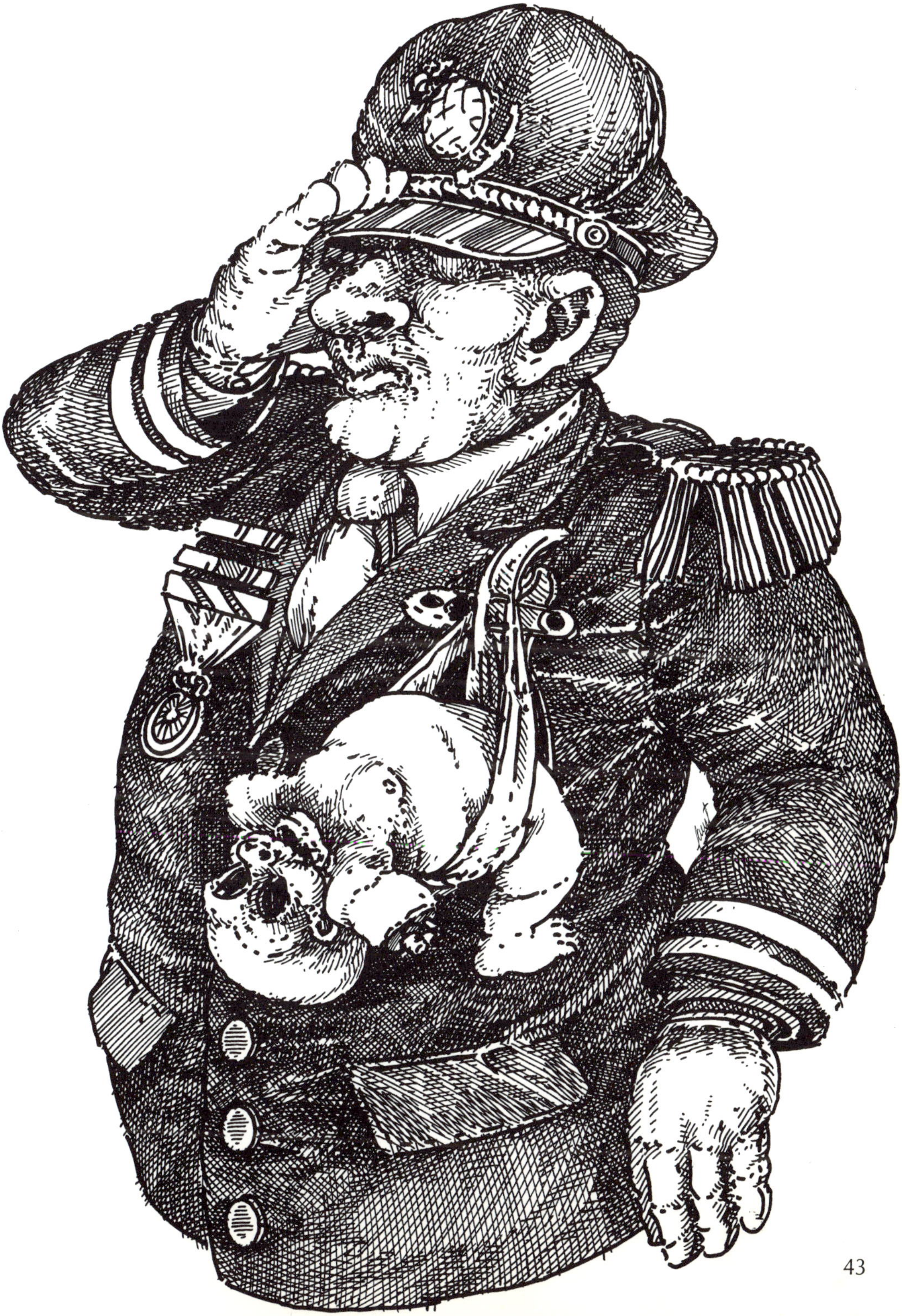

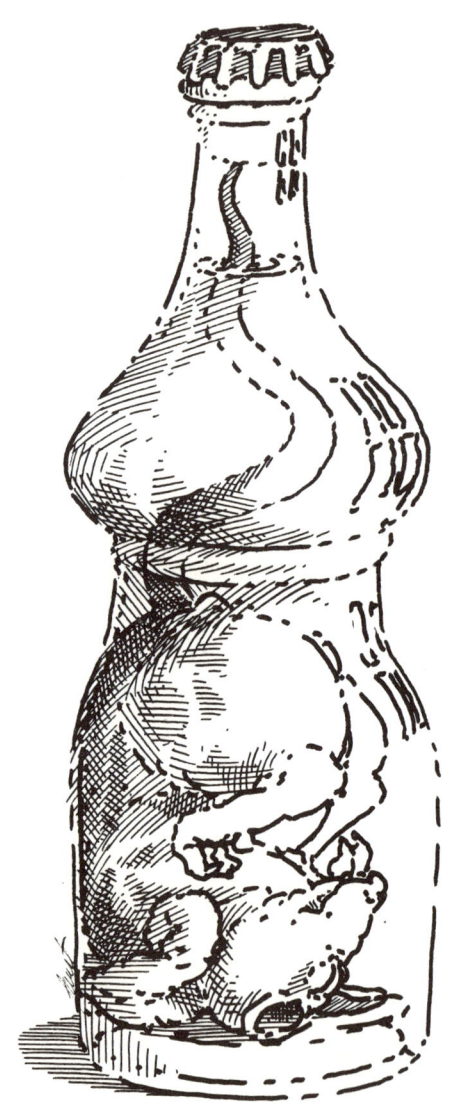

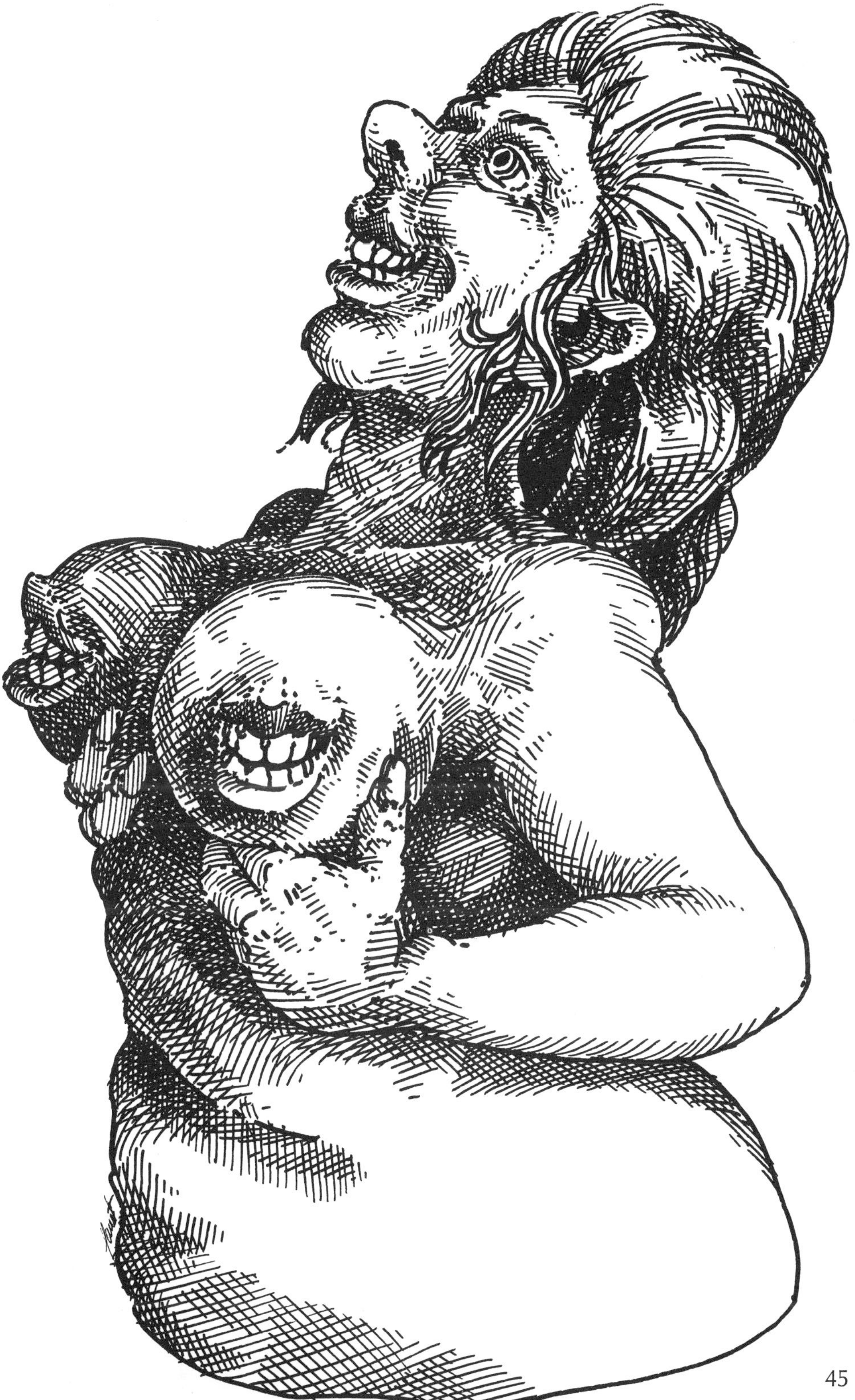

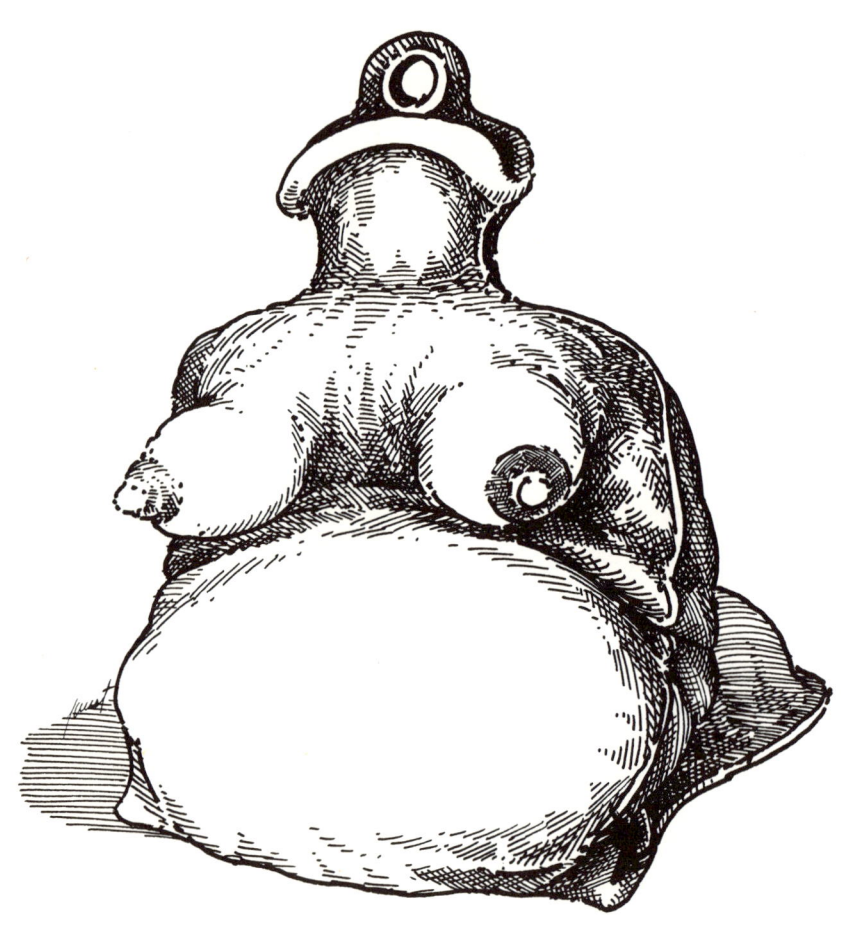

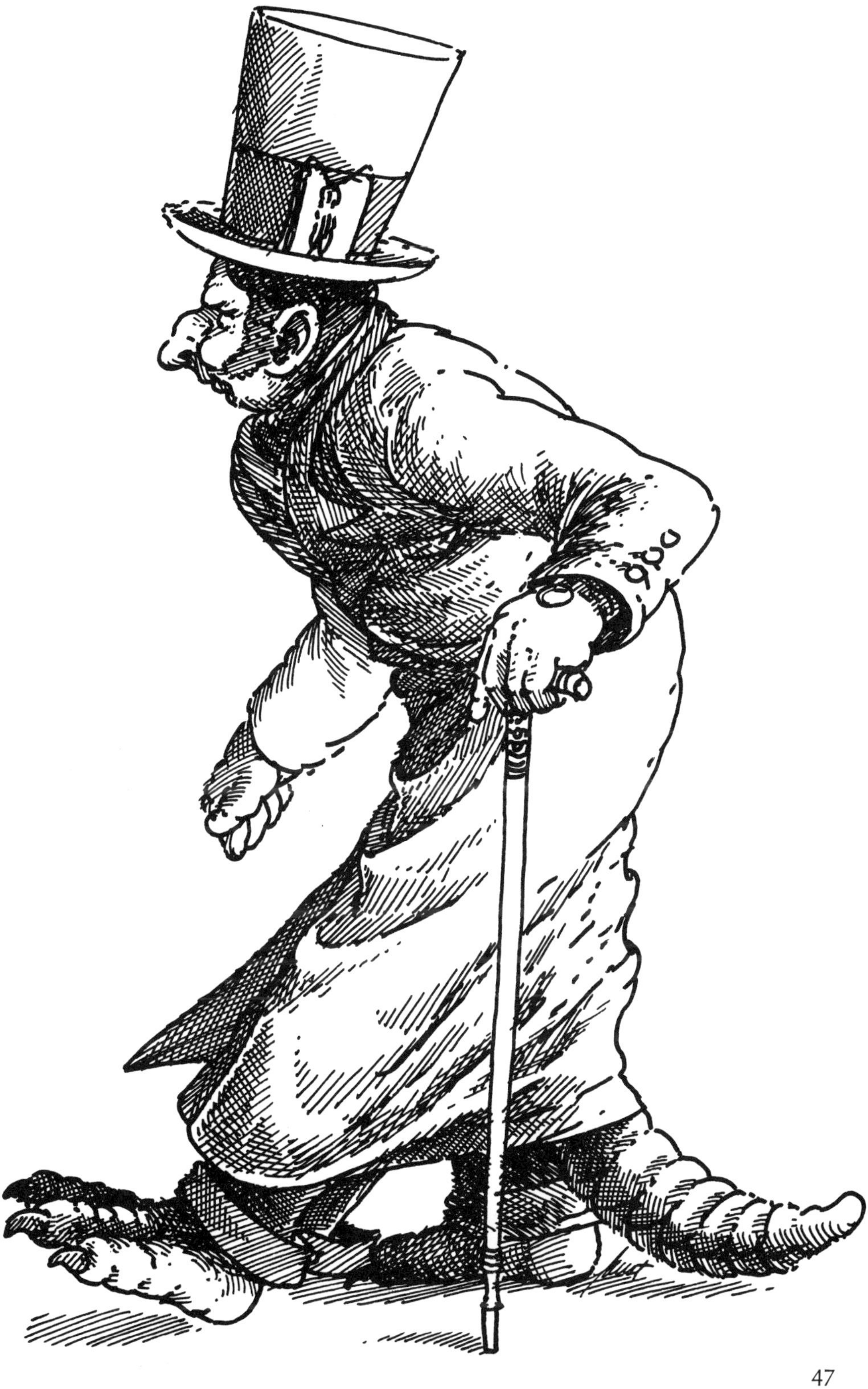

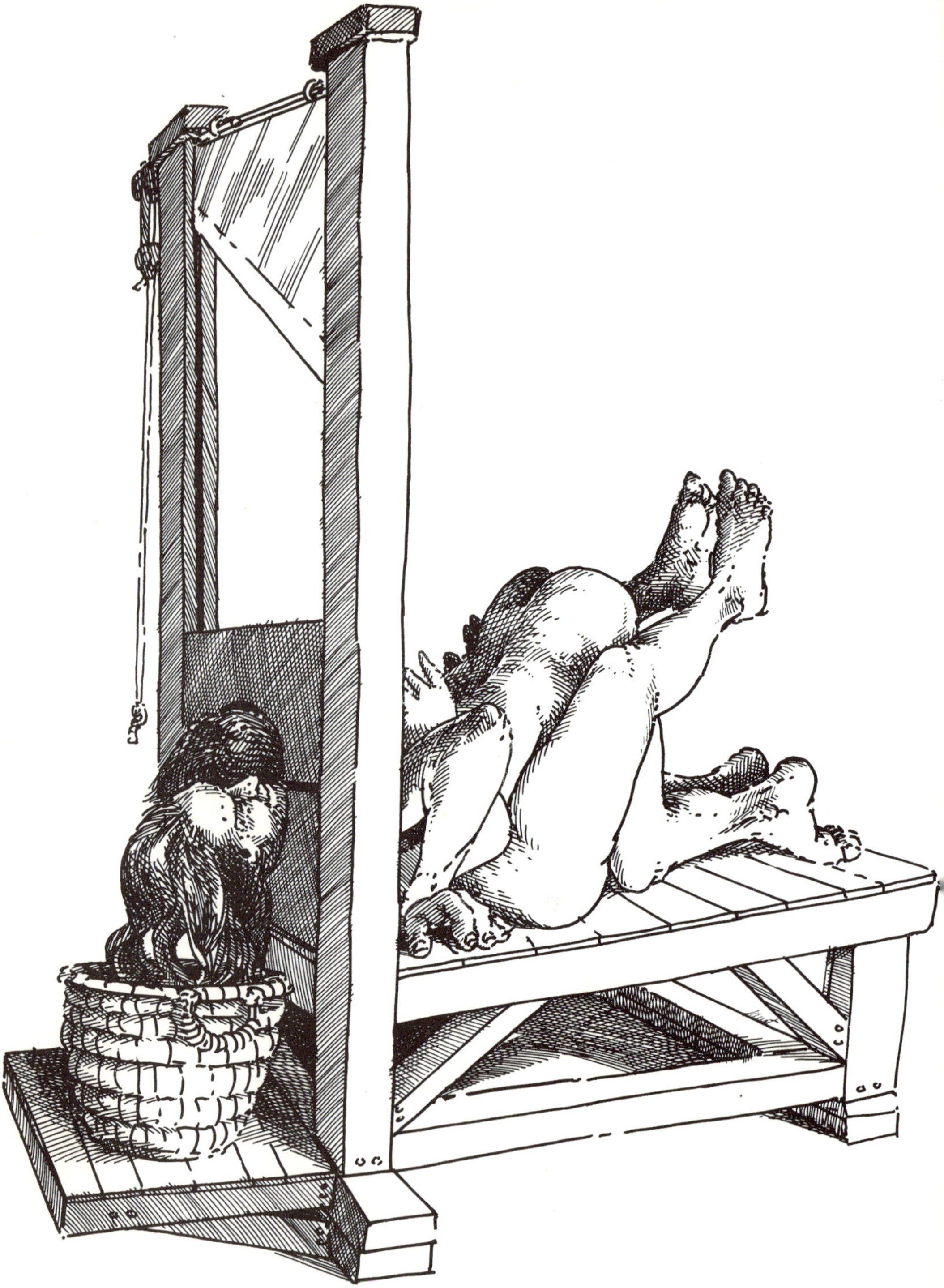

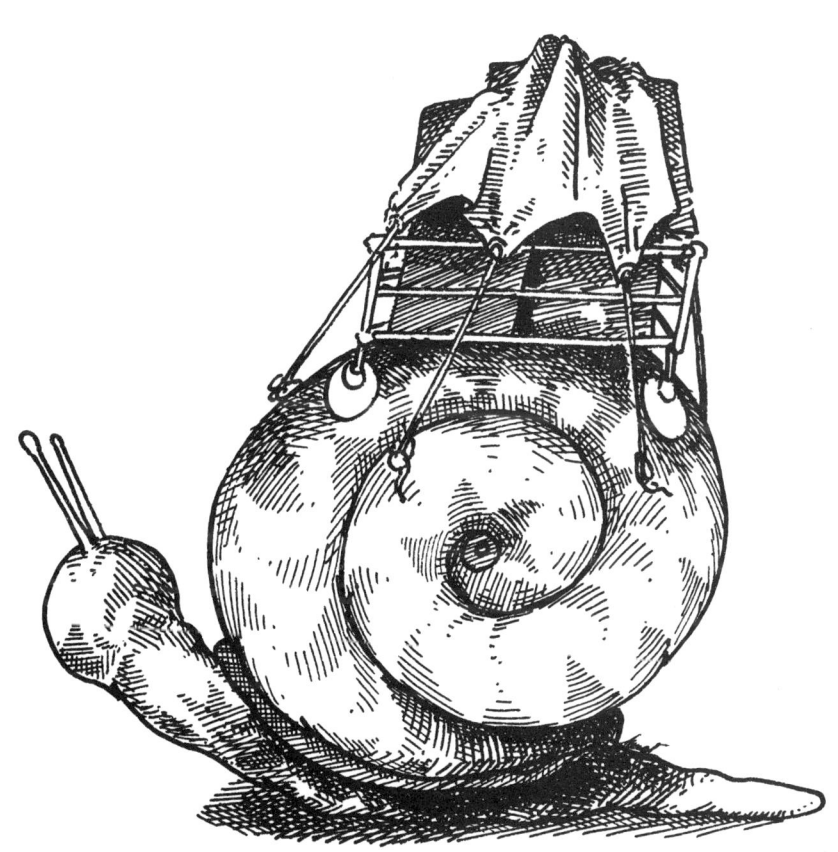

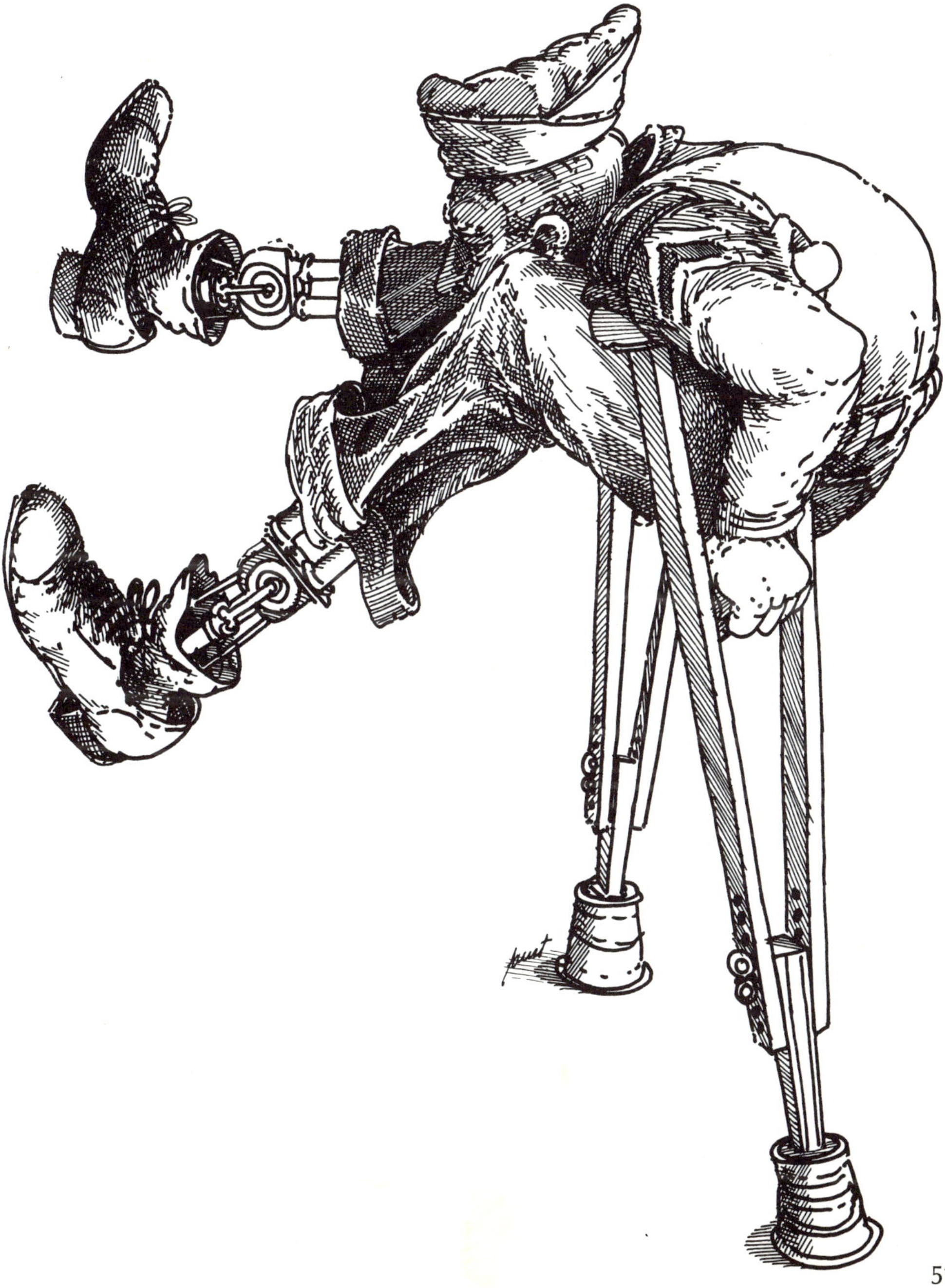

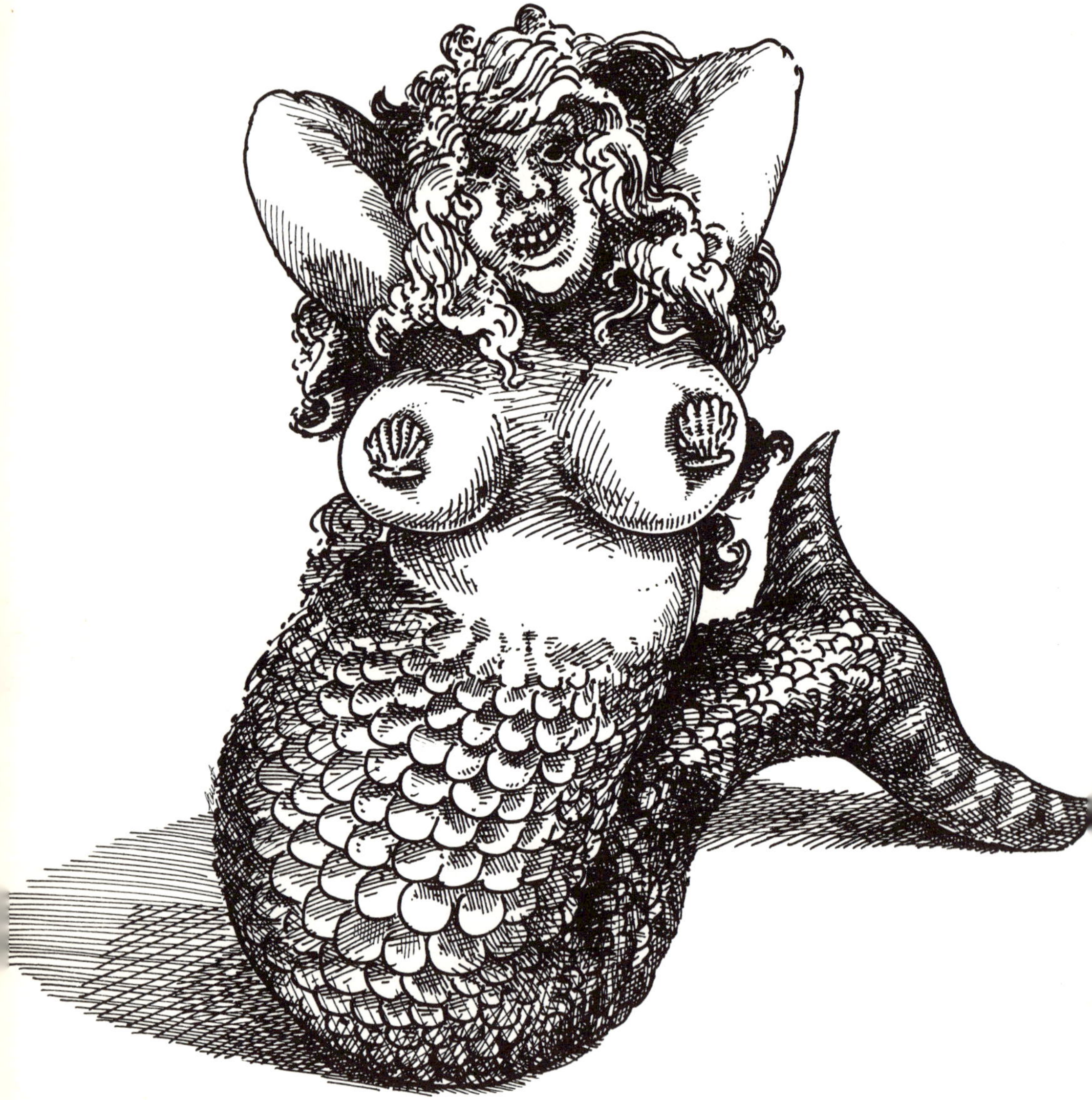

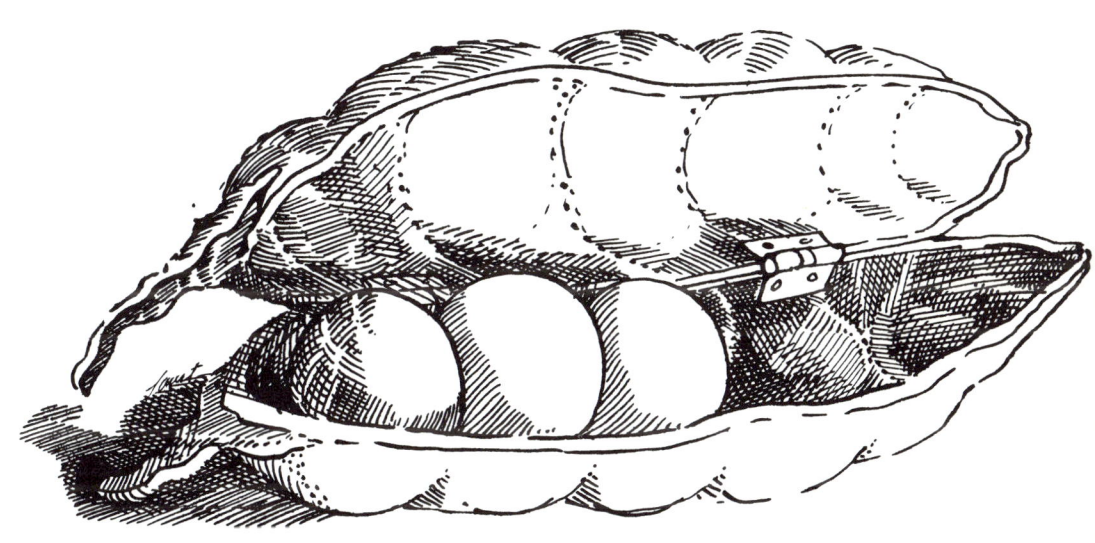

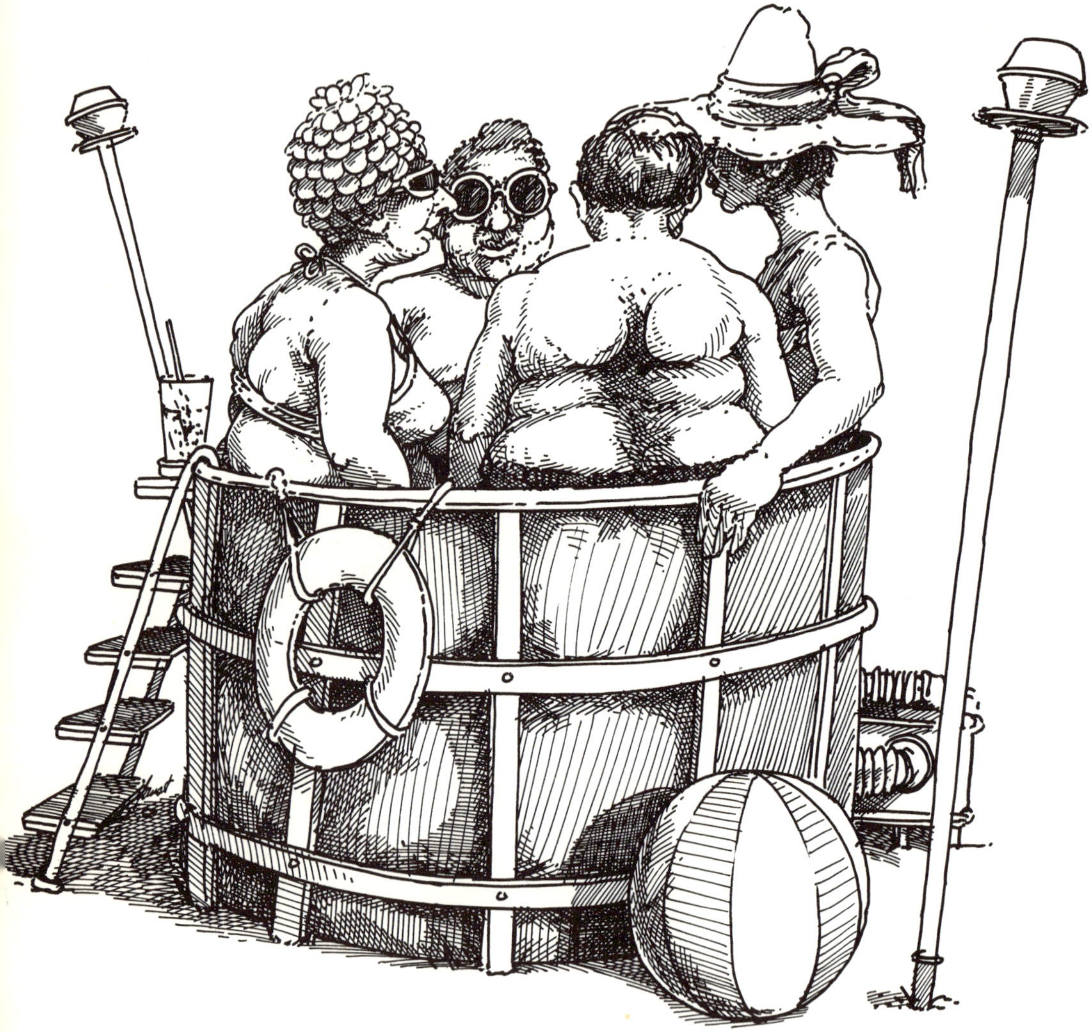

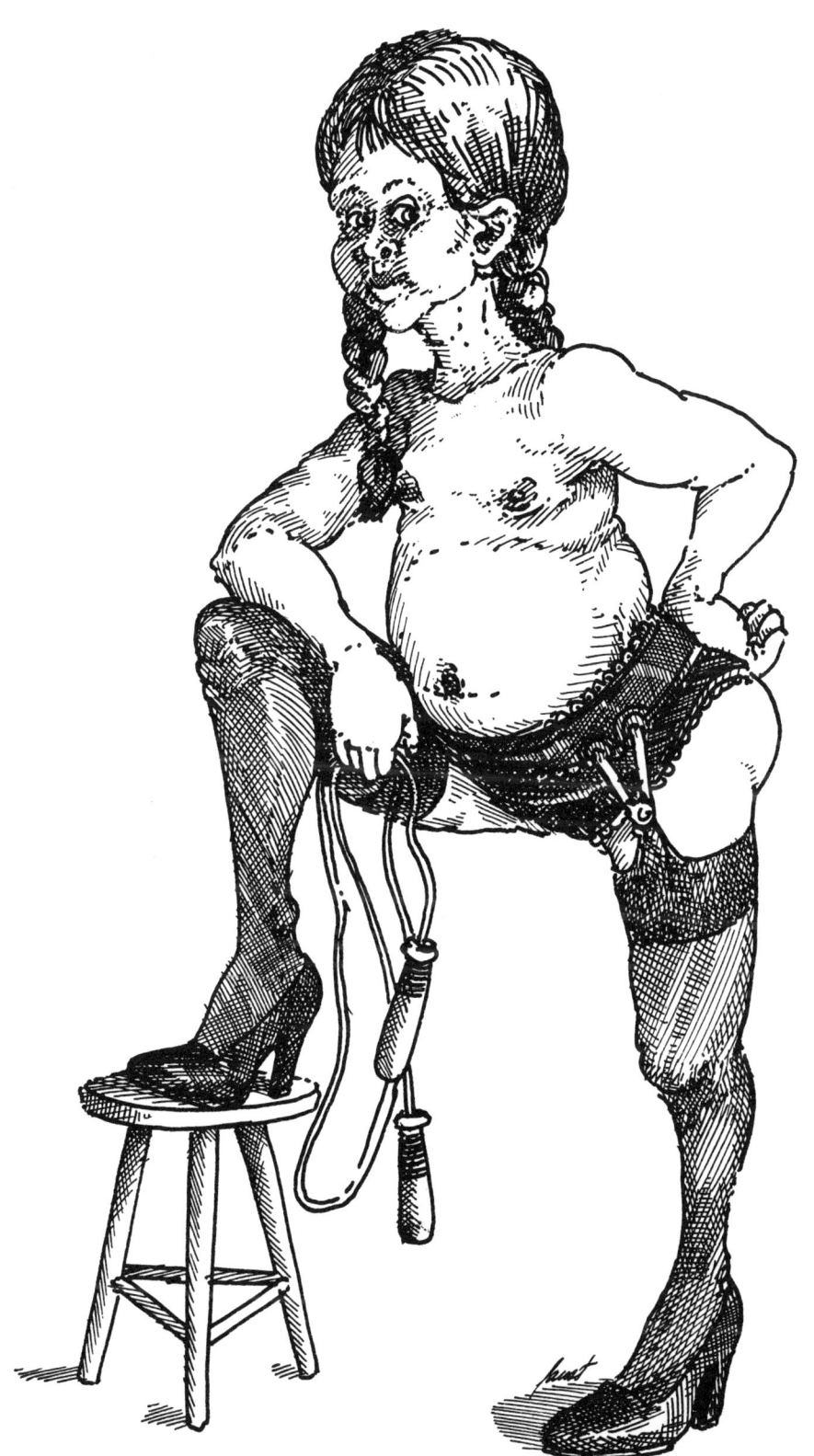

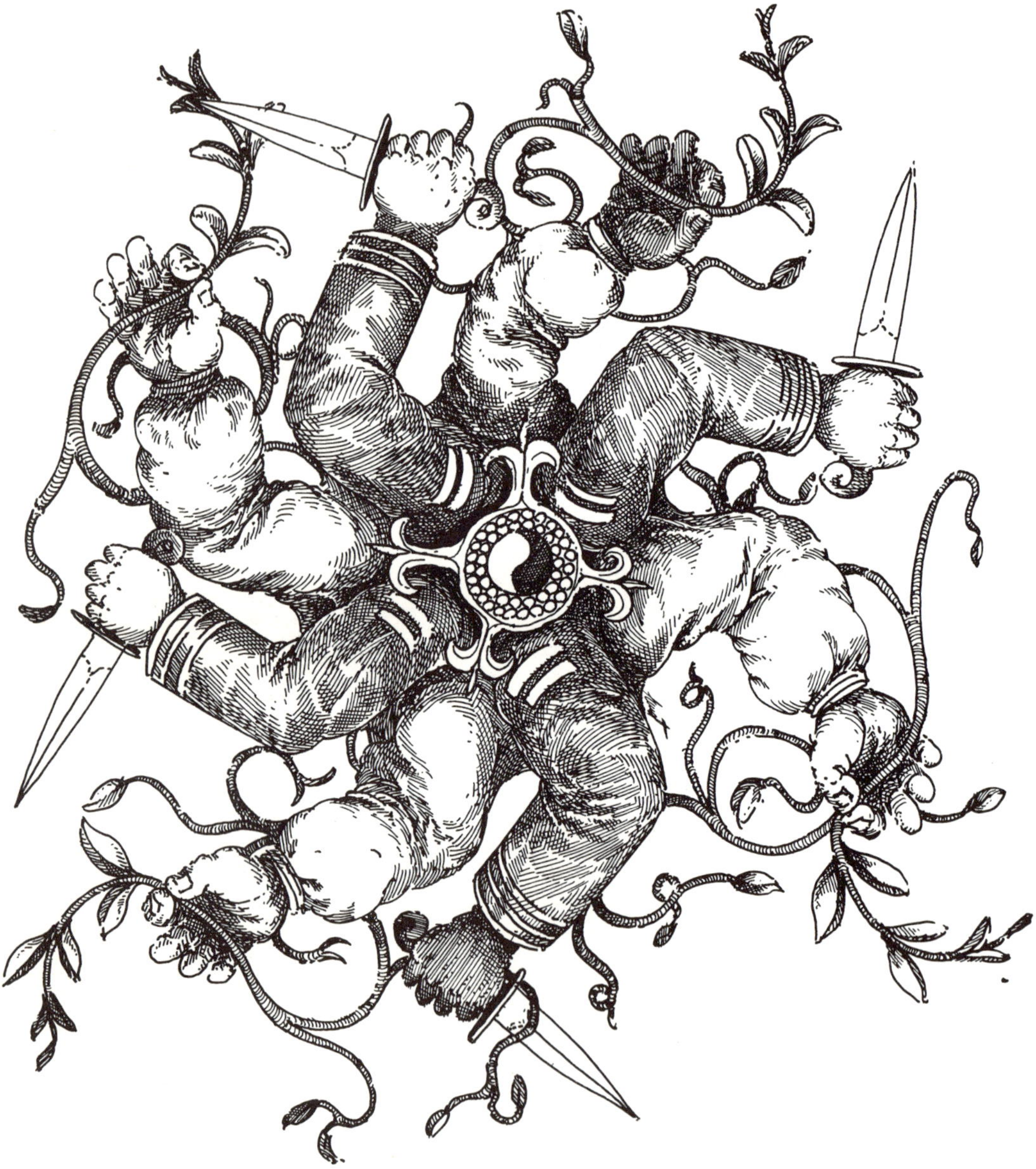

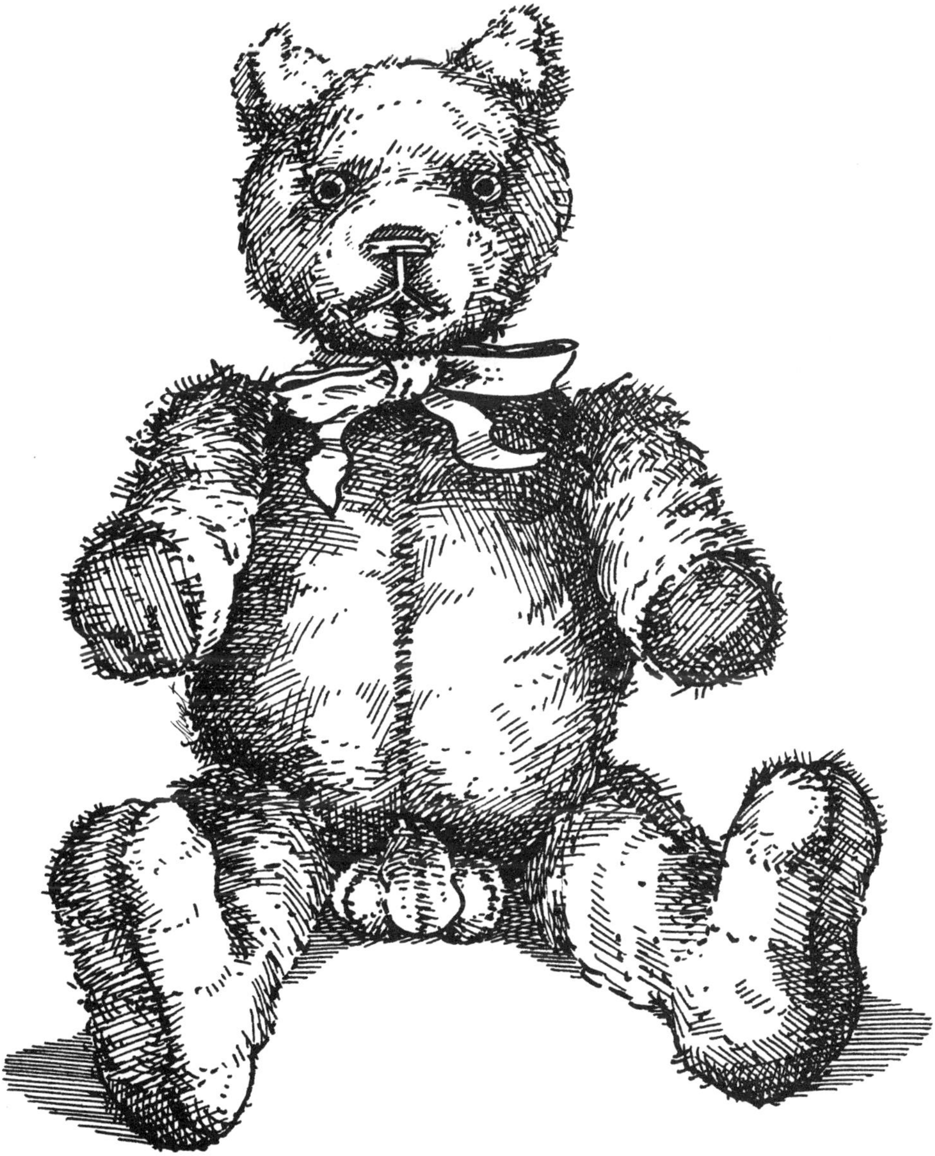

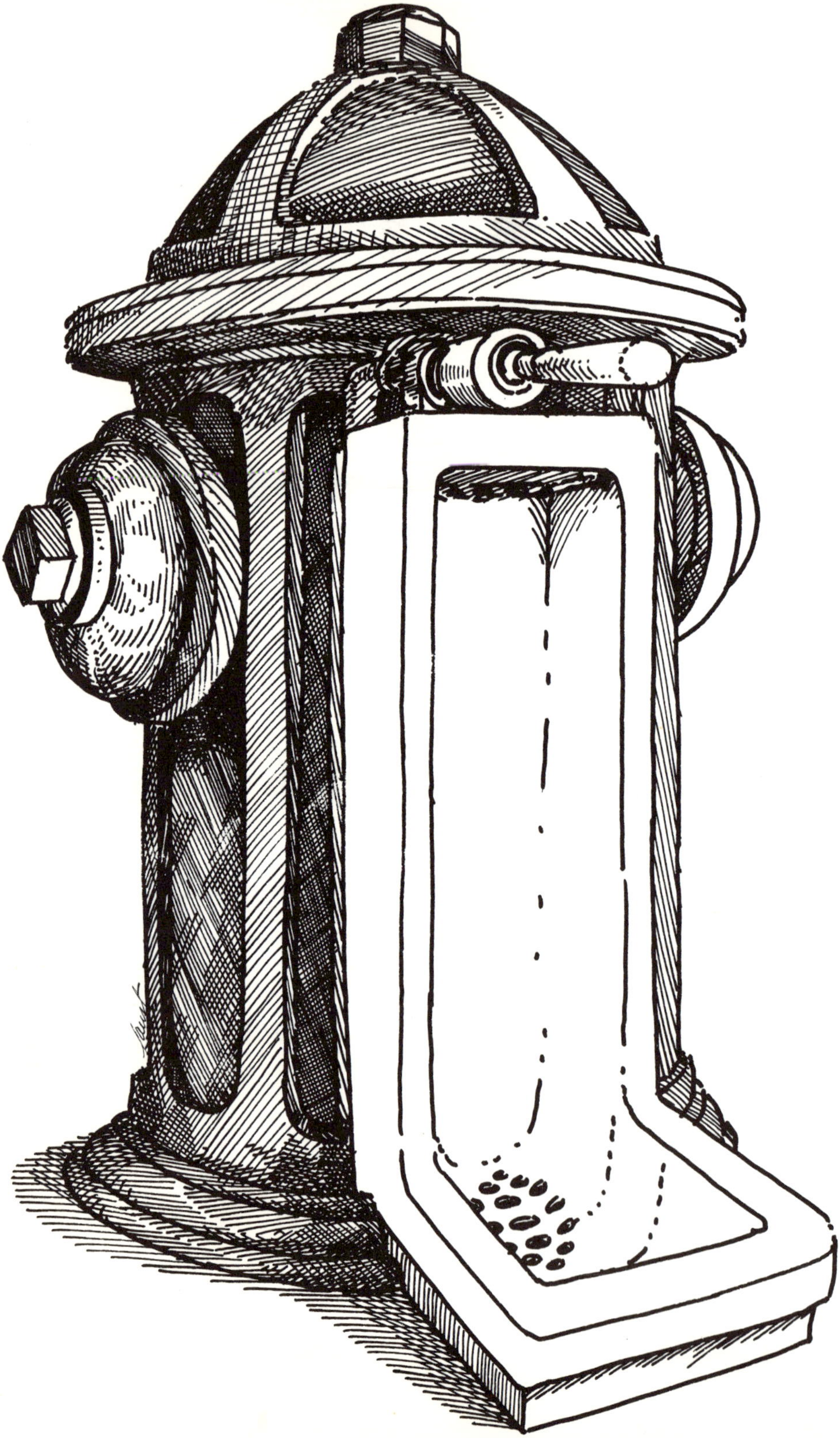

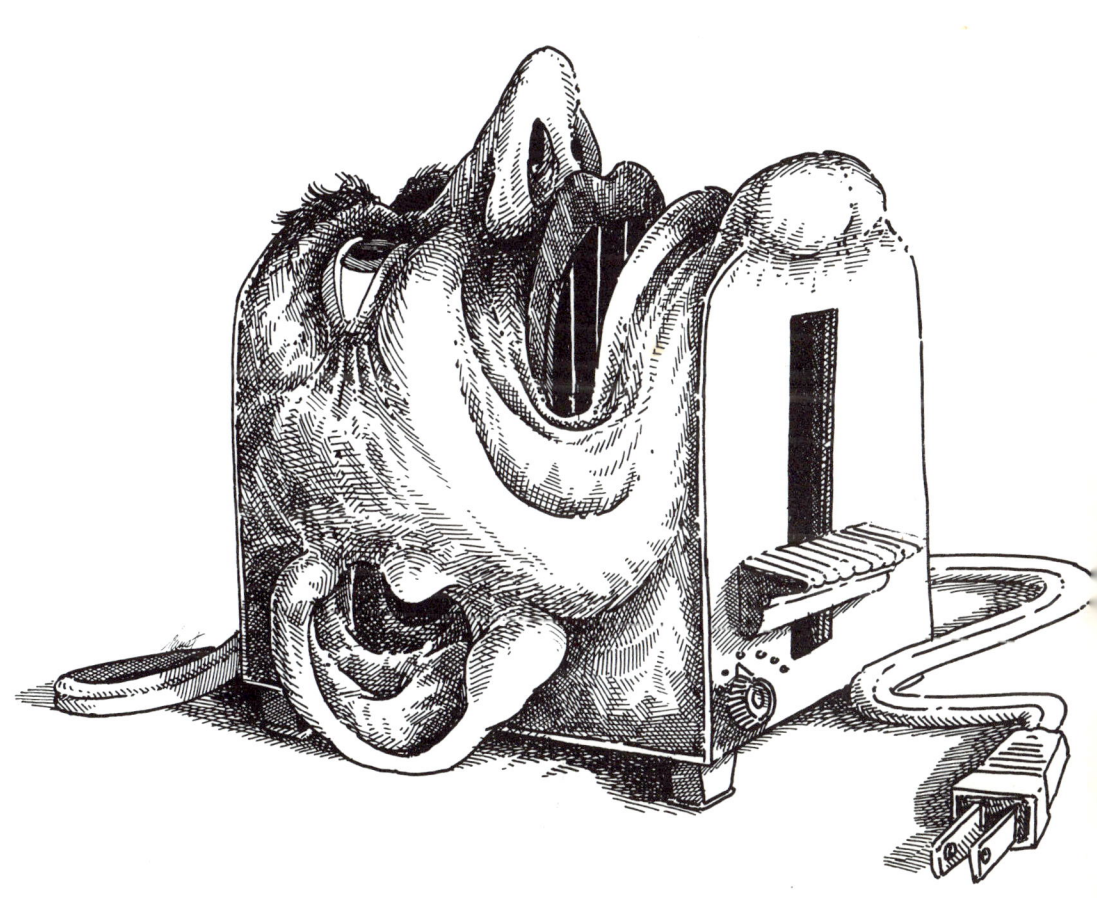

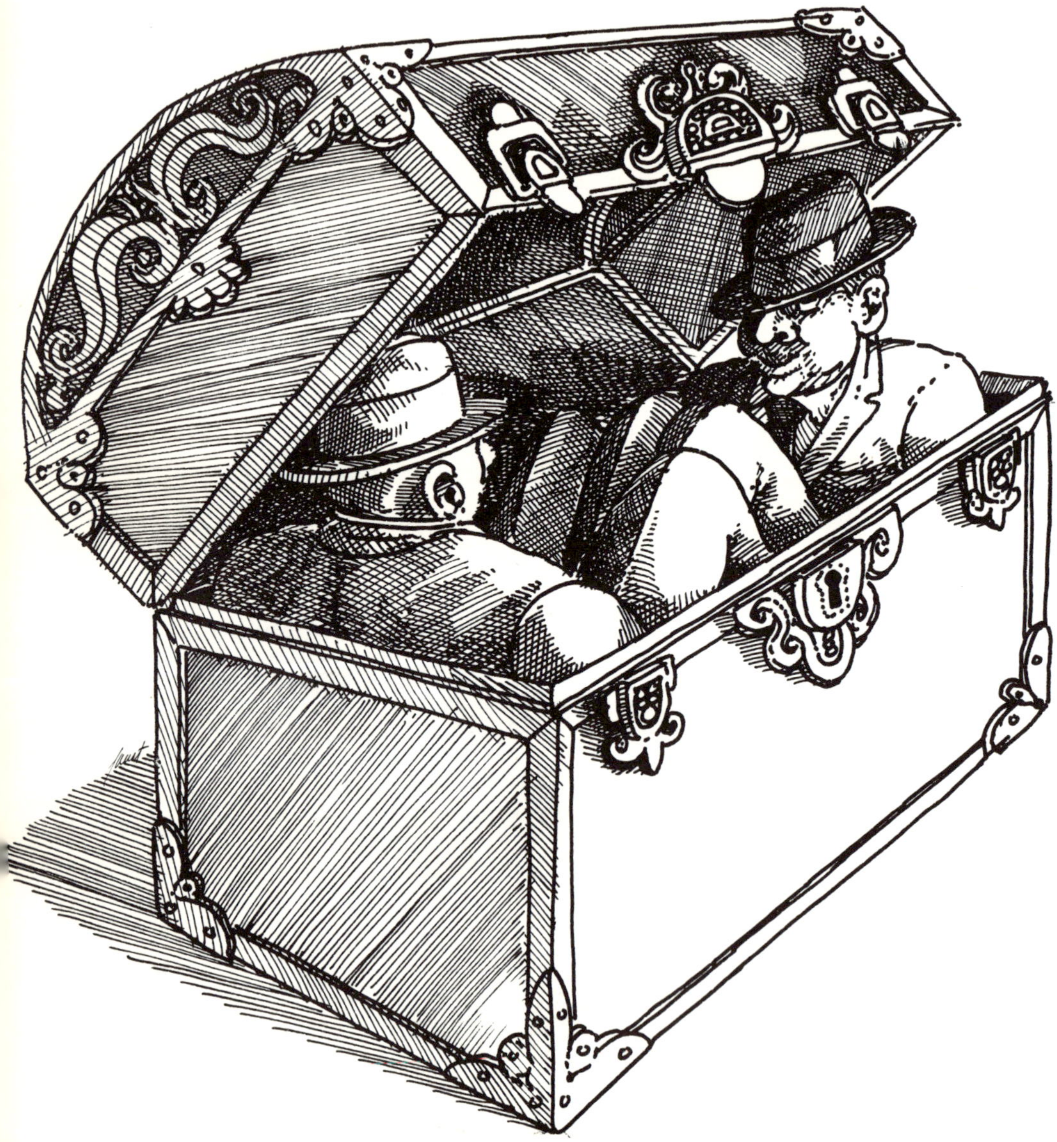

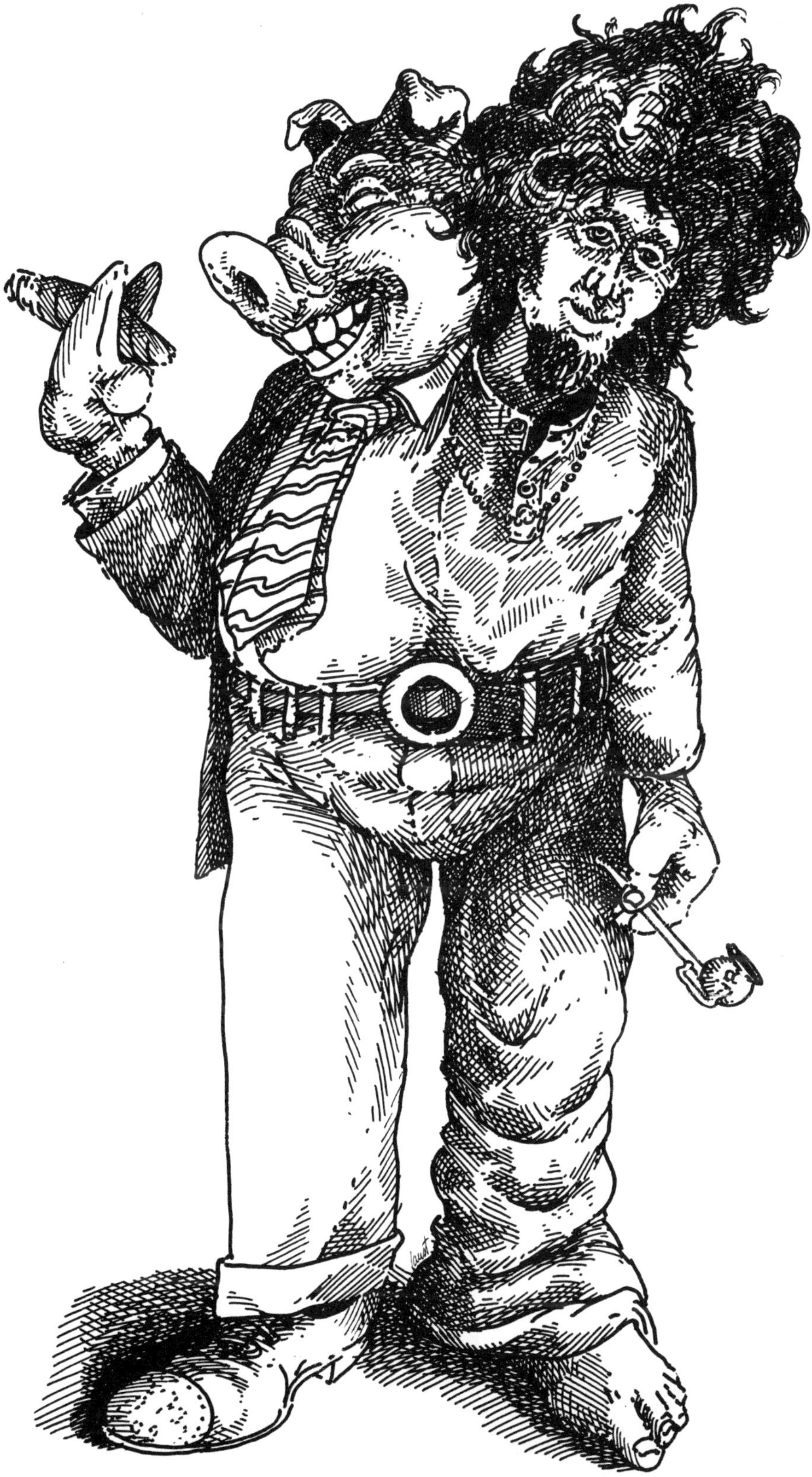

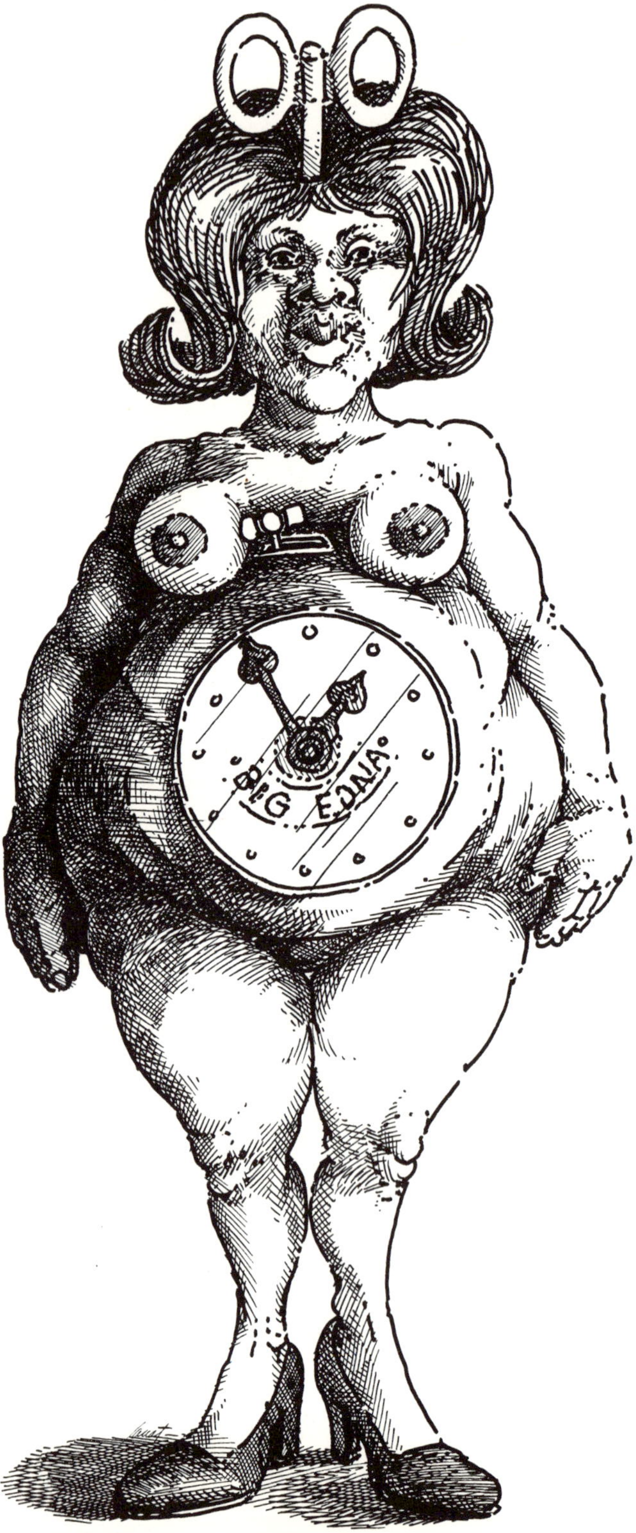
BIG EDNA

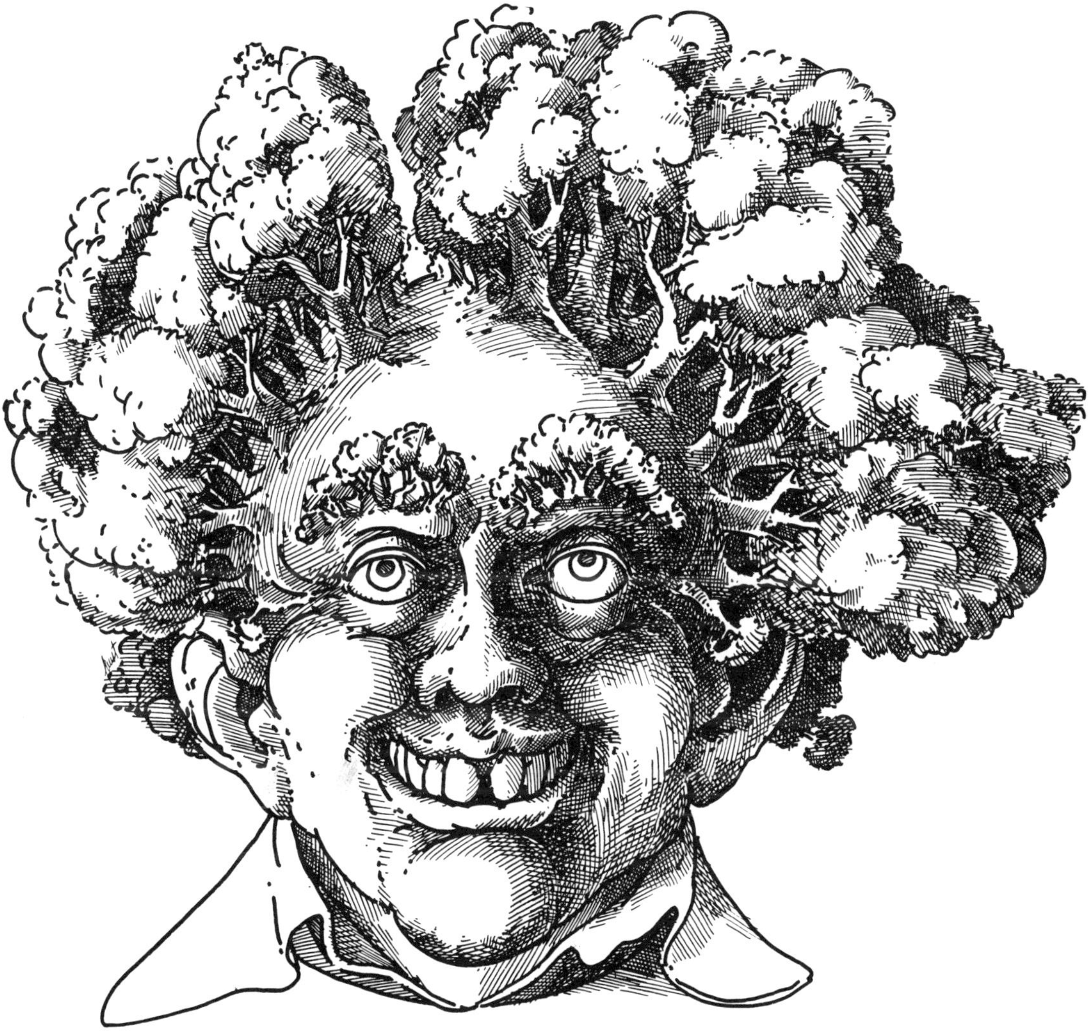

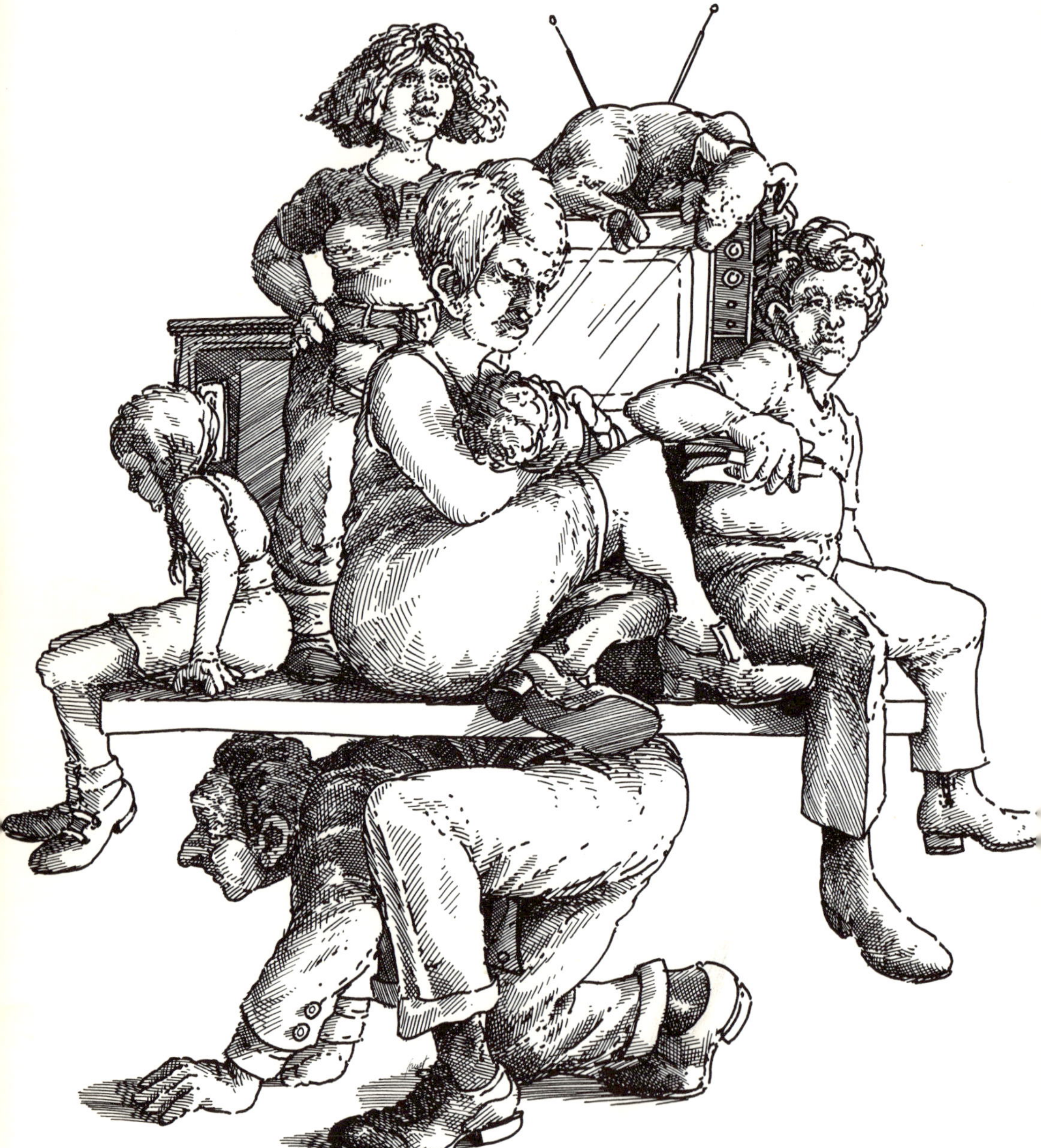

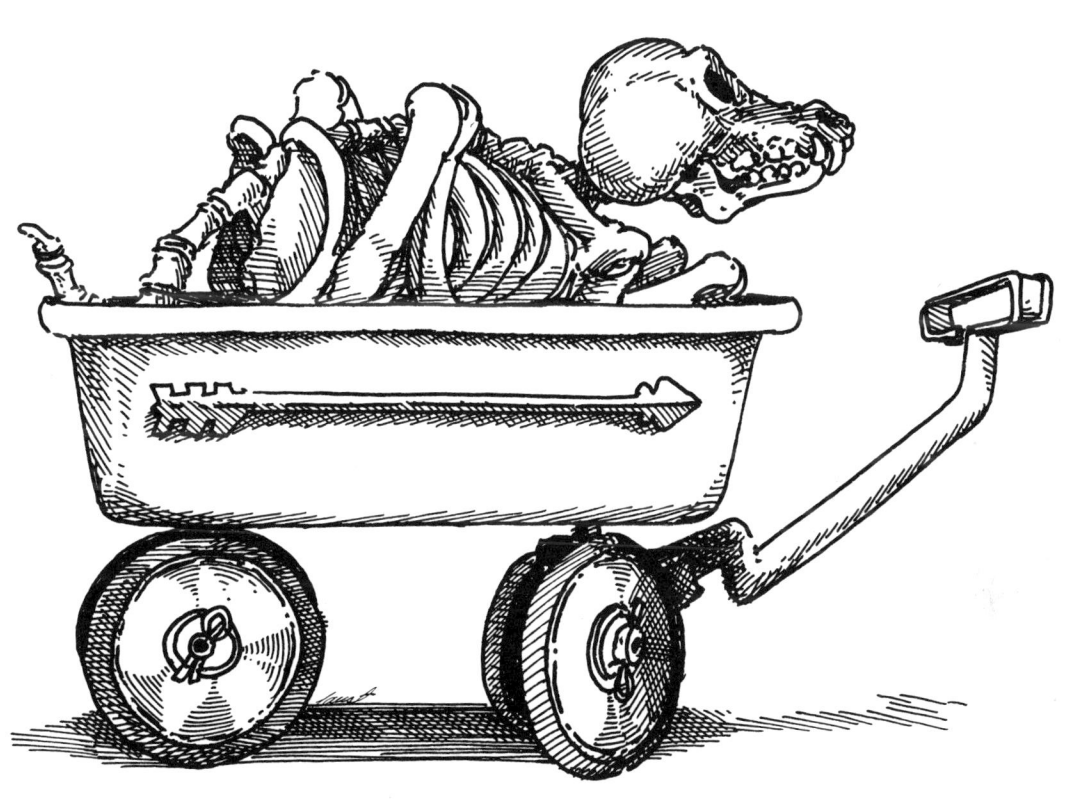

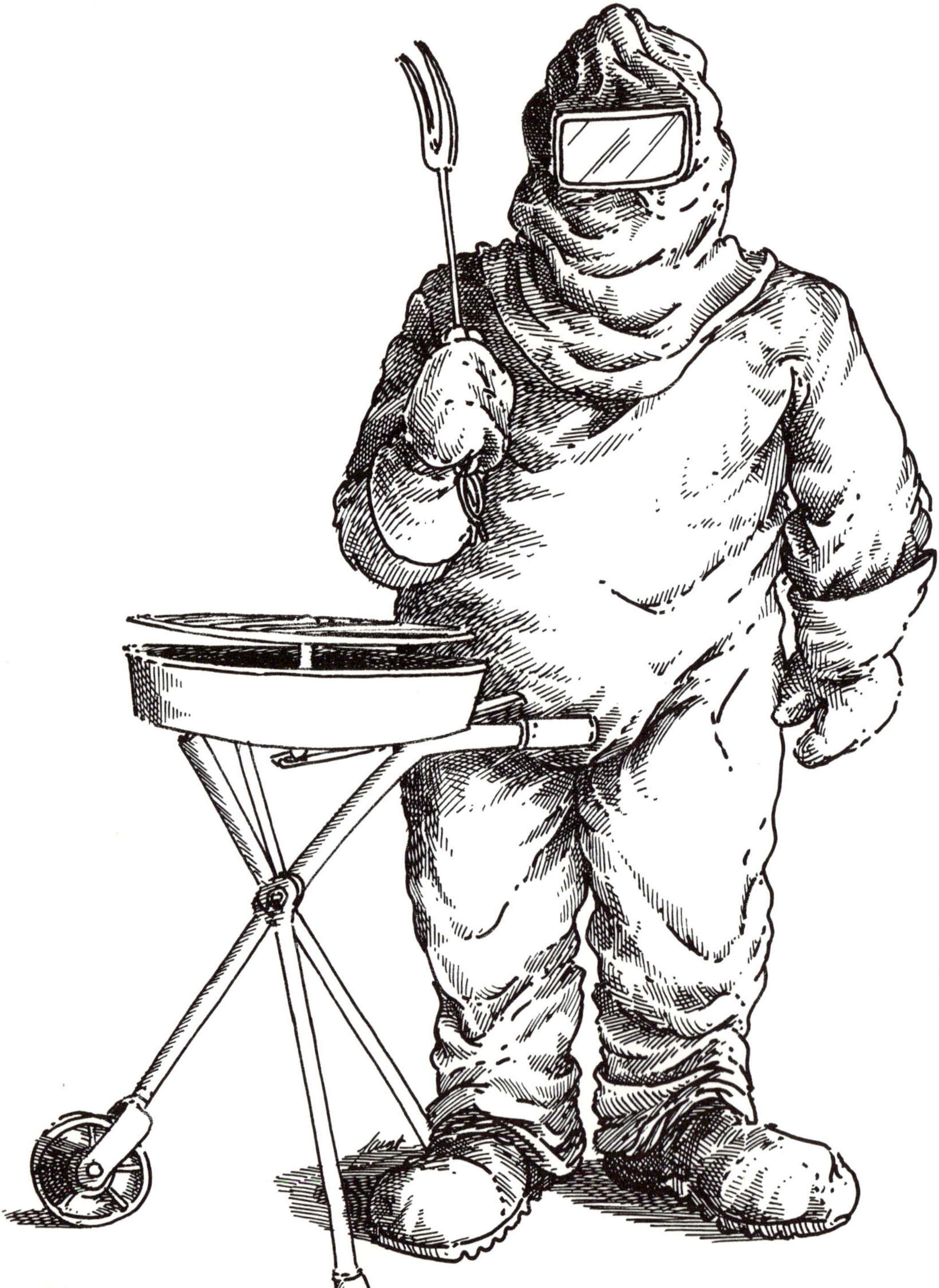

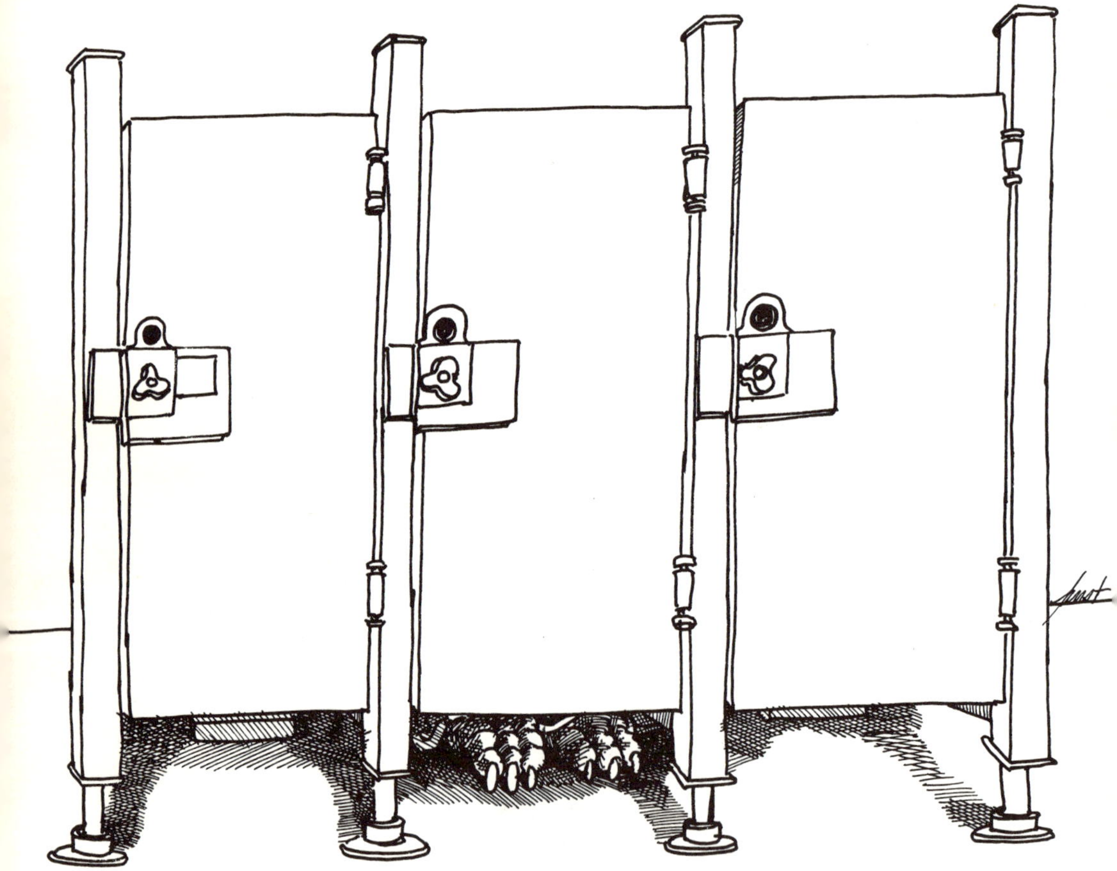

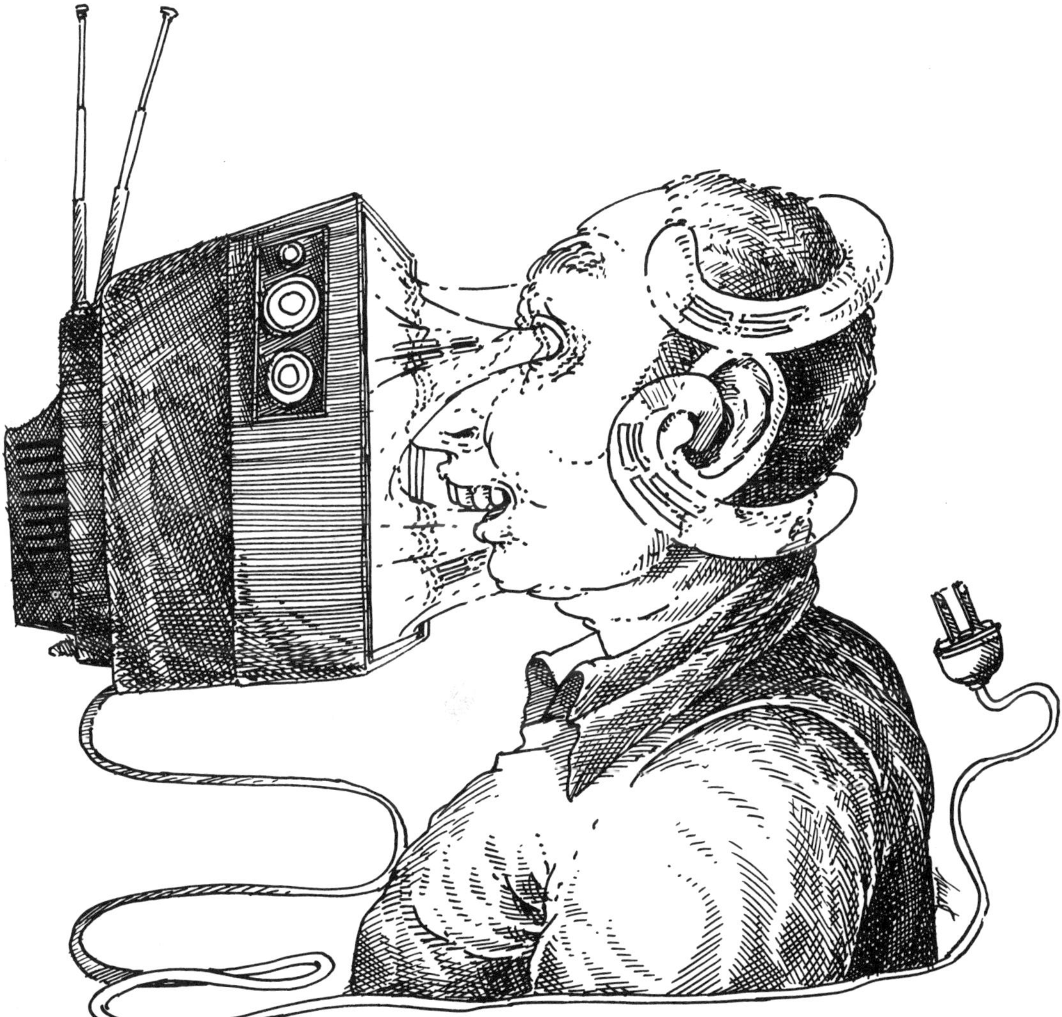

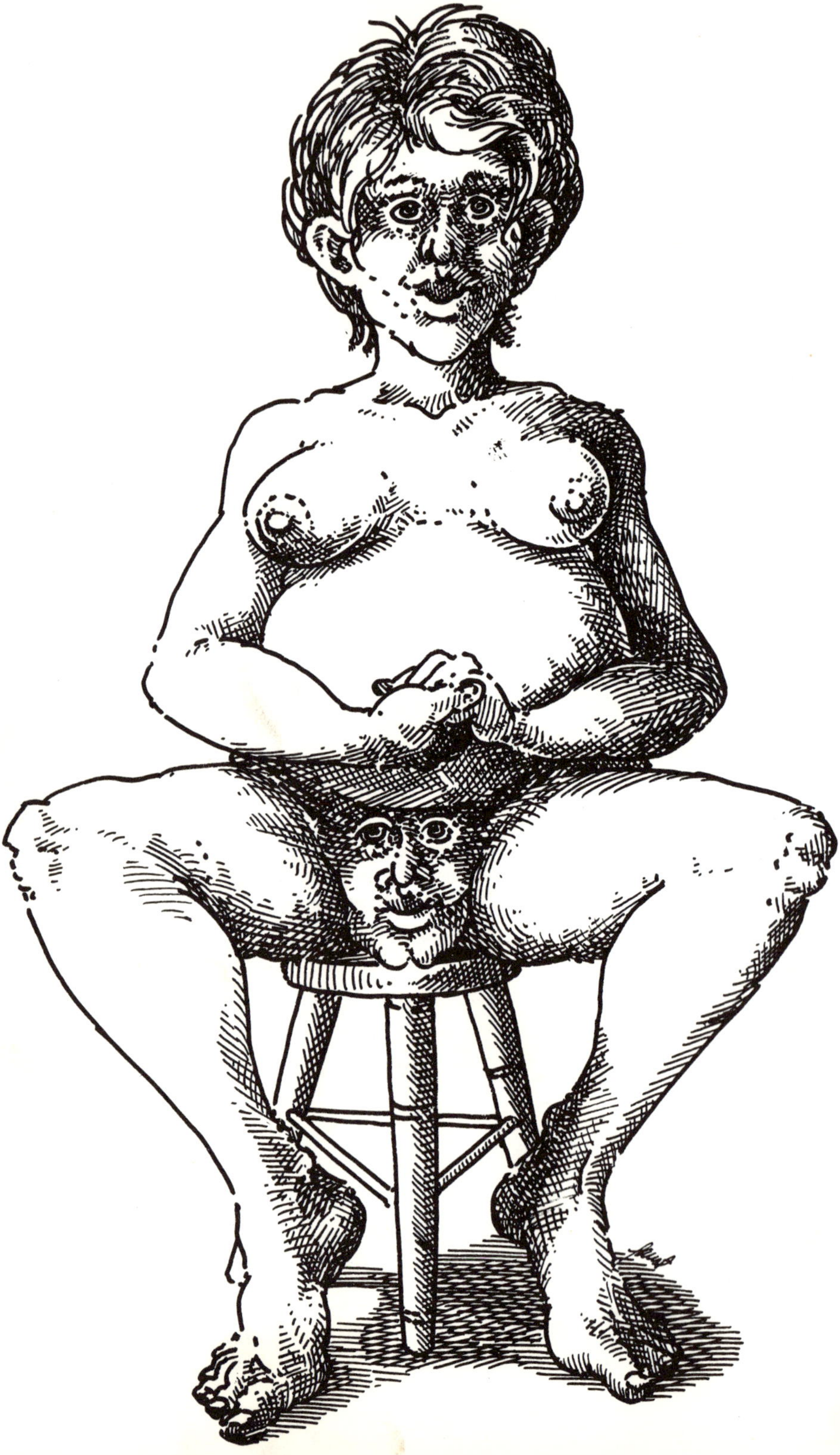

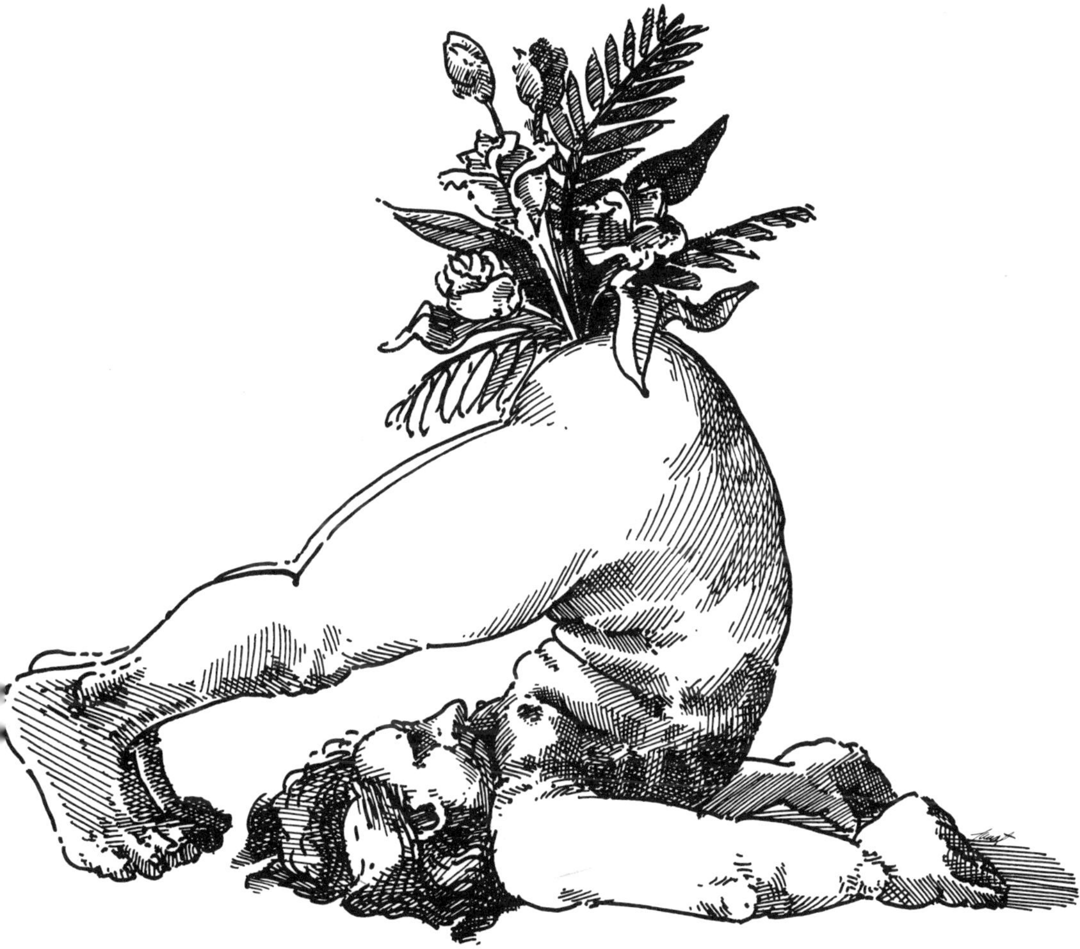

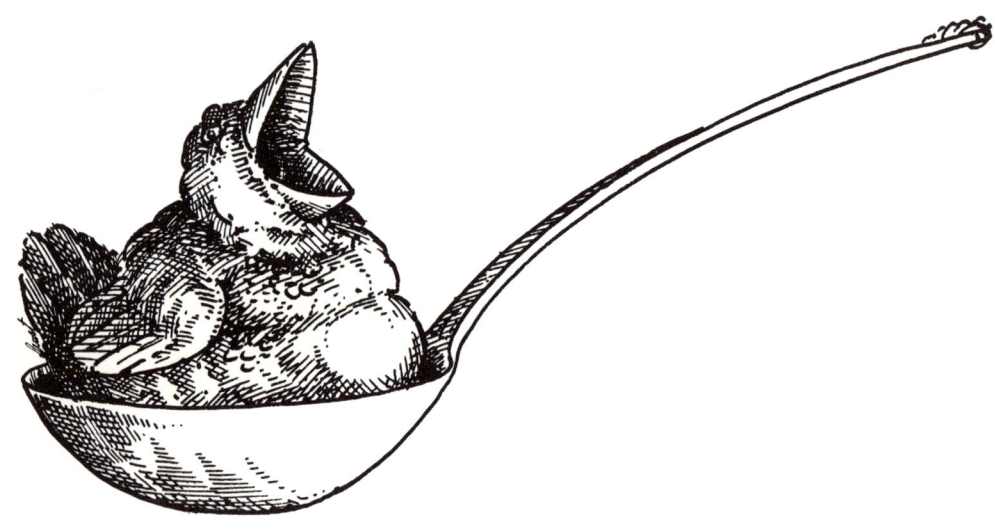

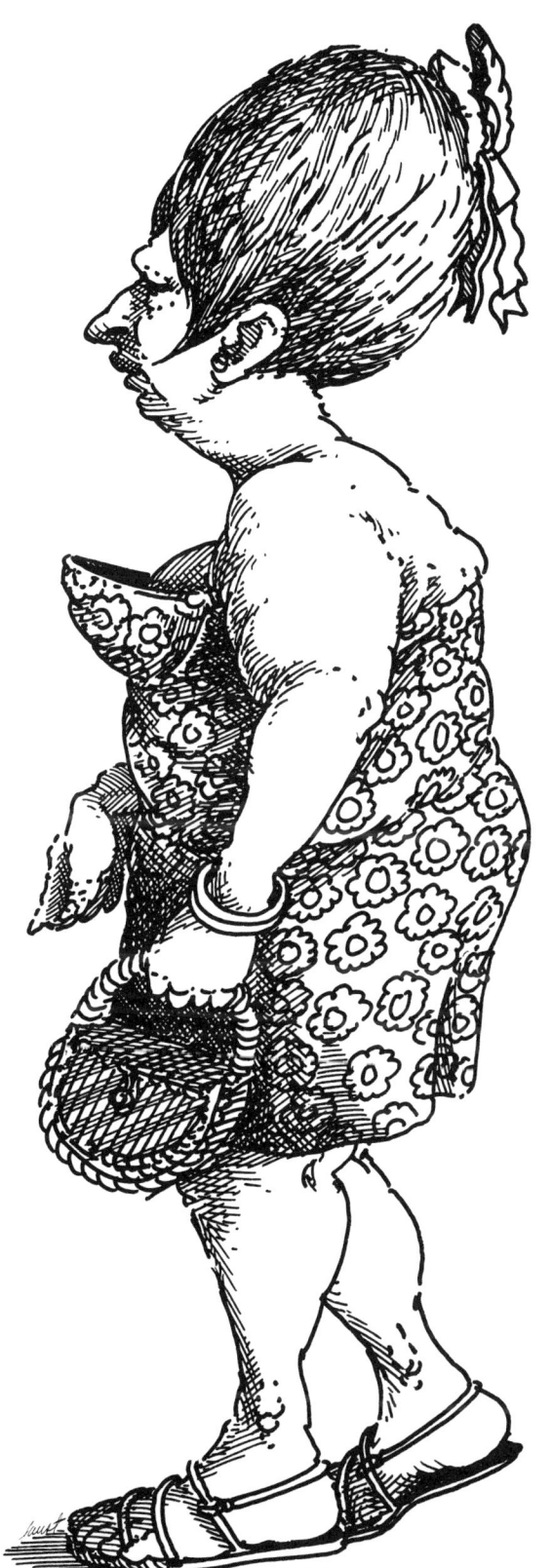

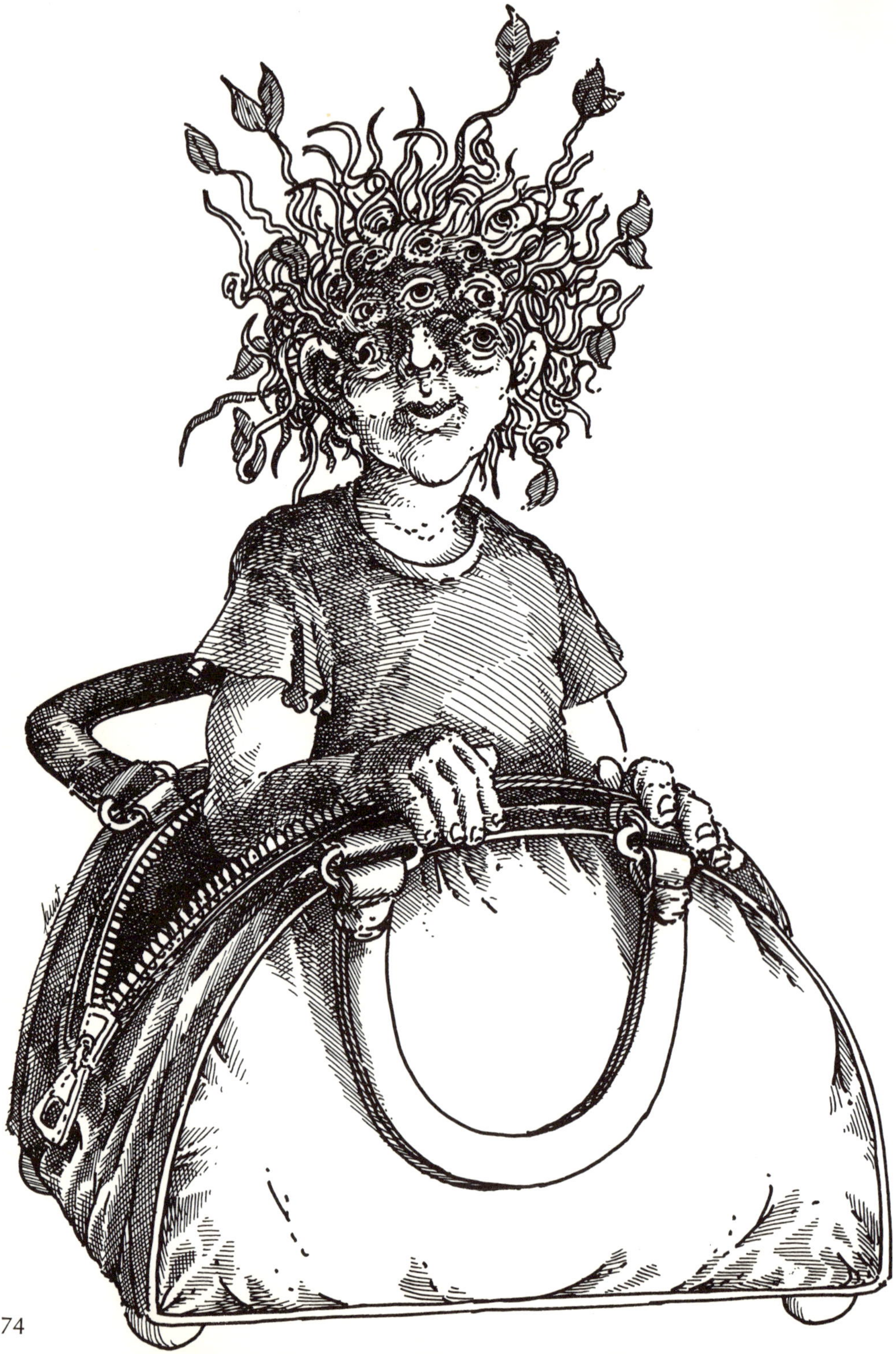

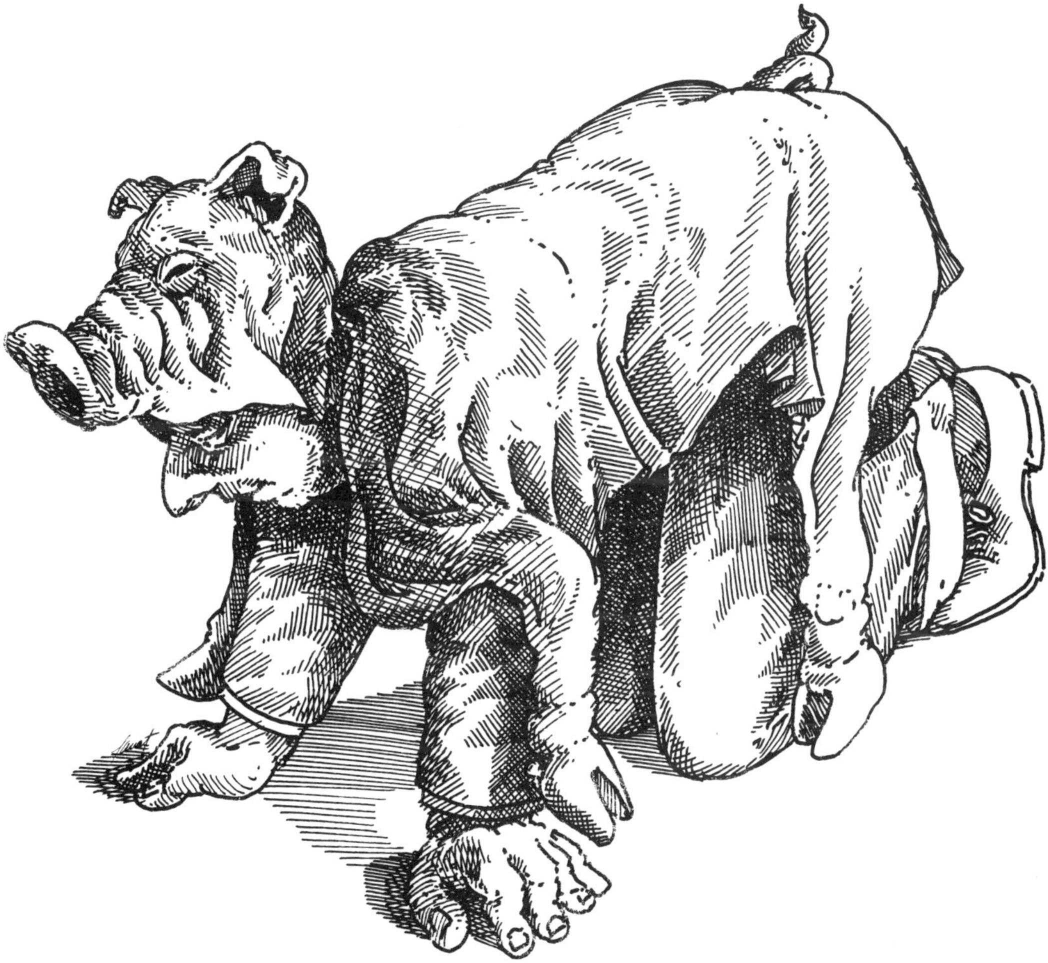

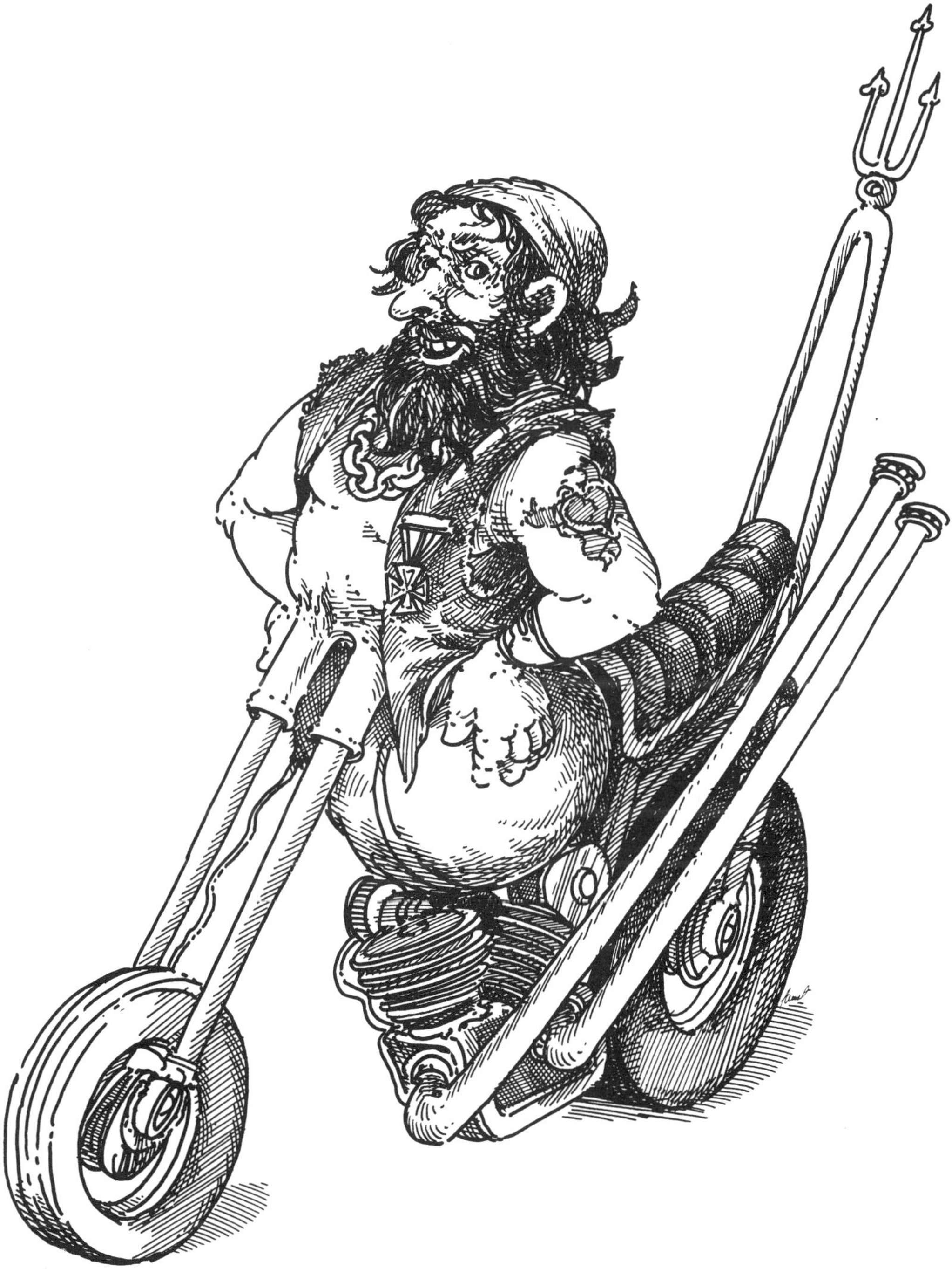

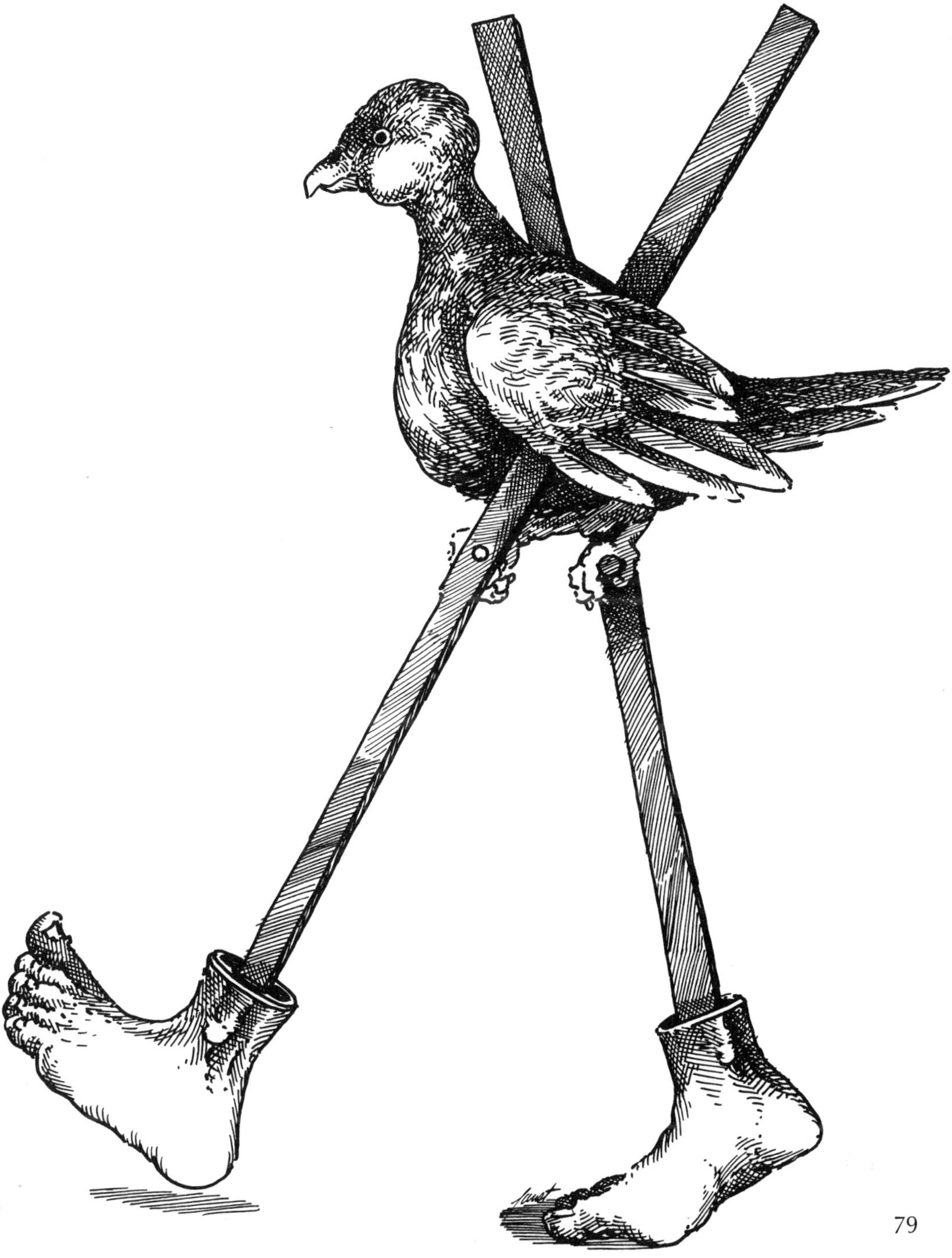

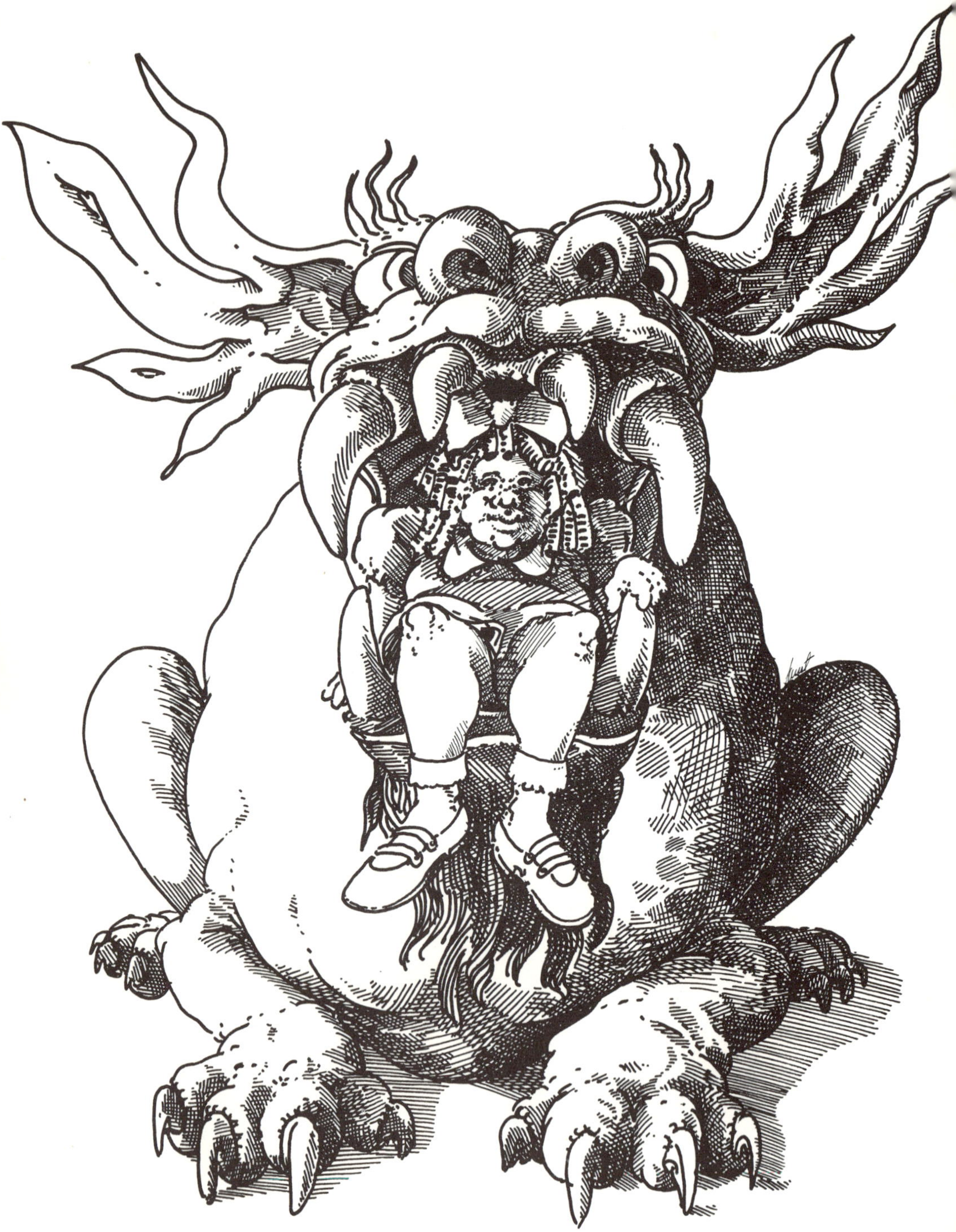

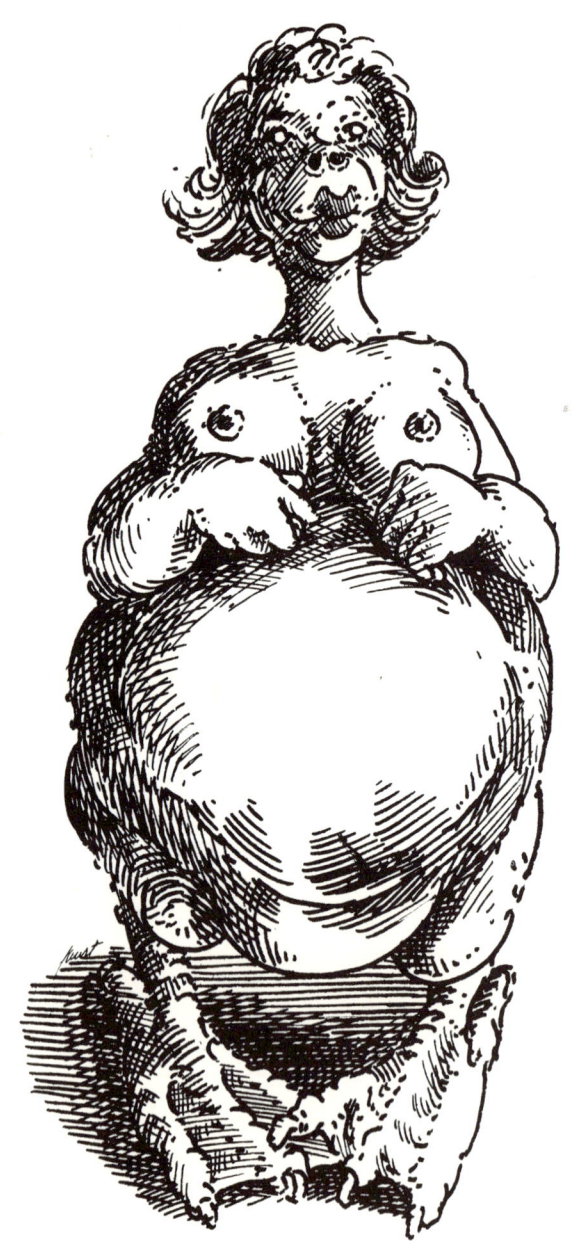

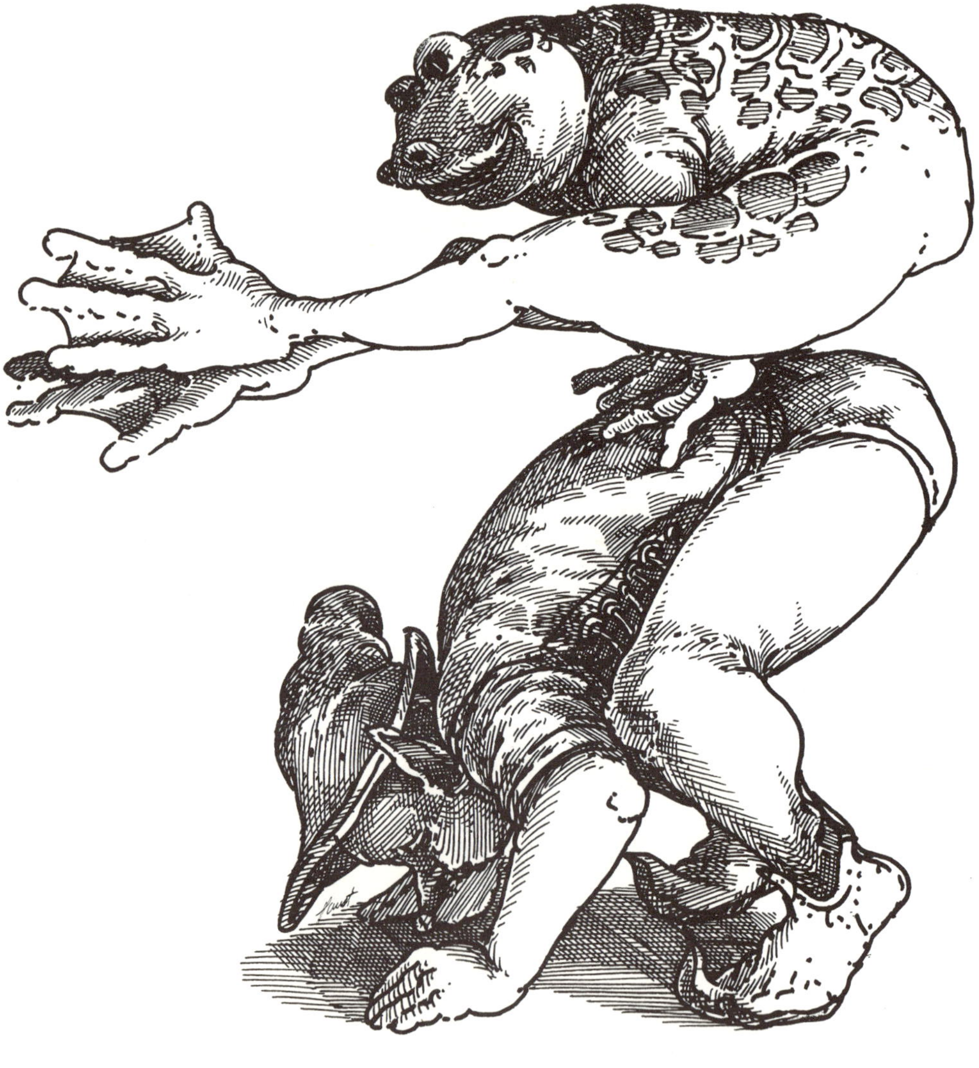

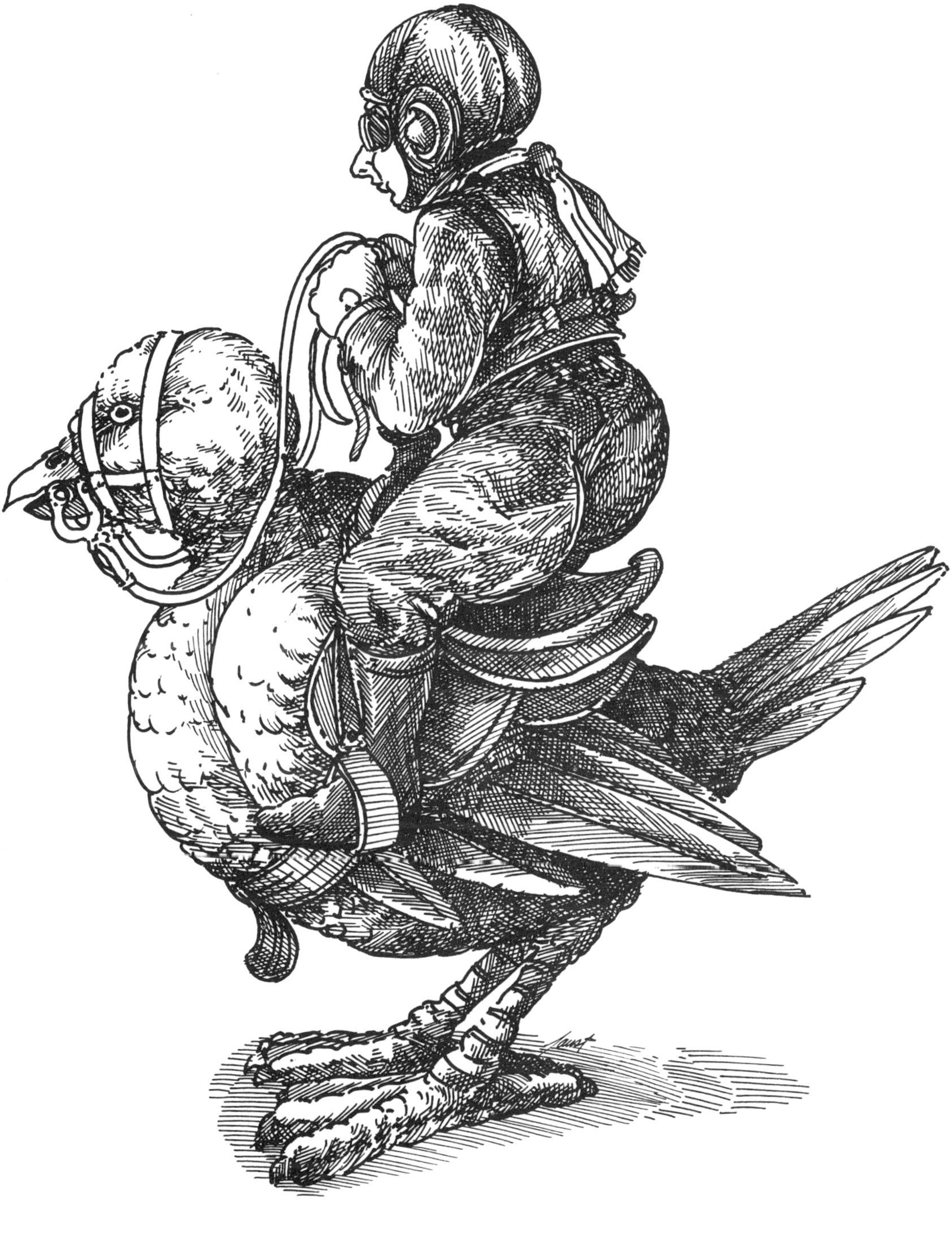

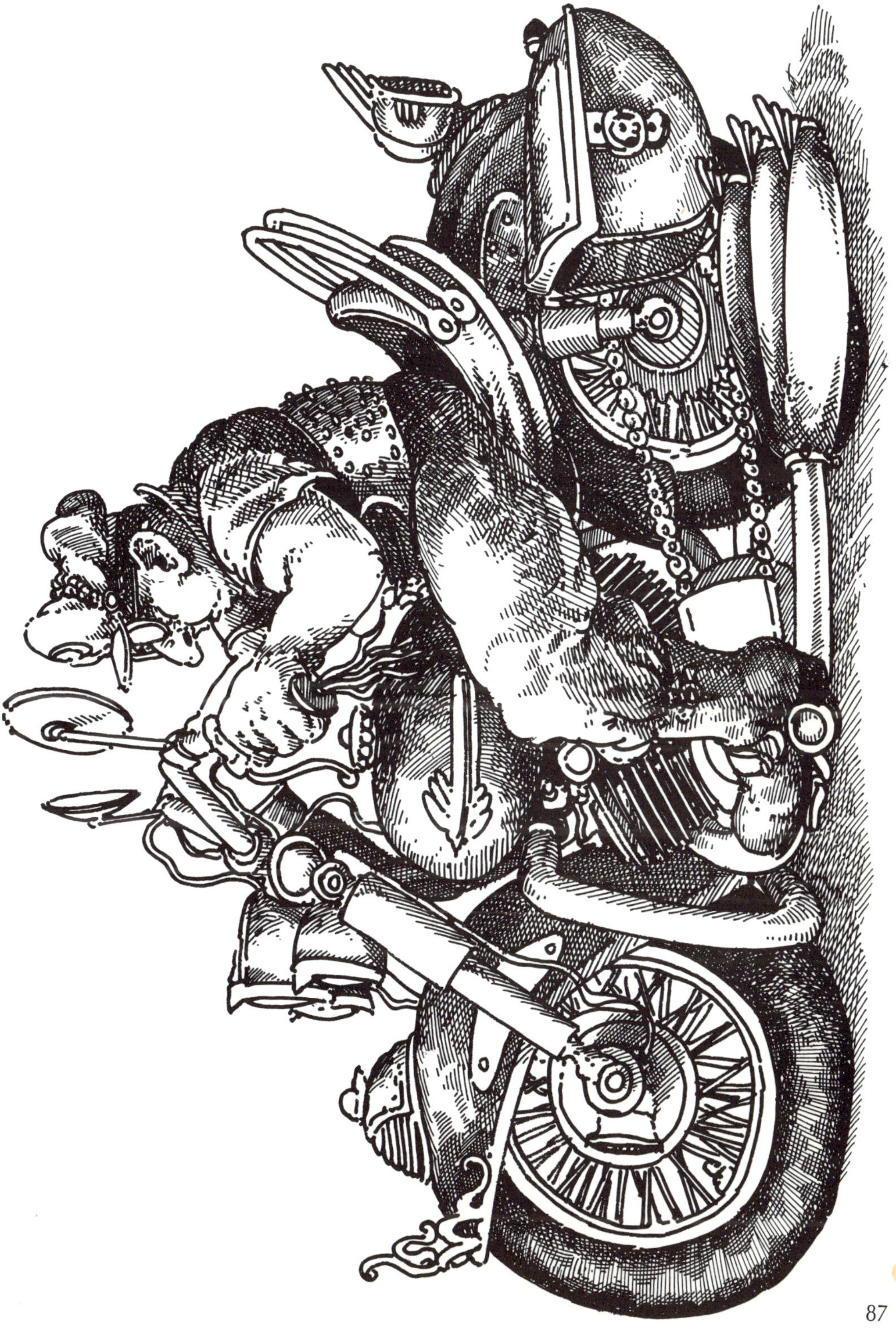

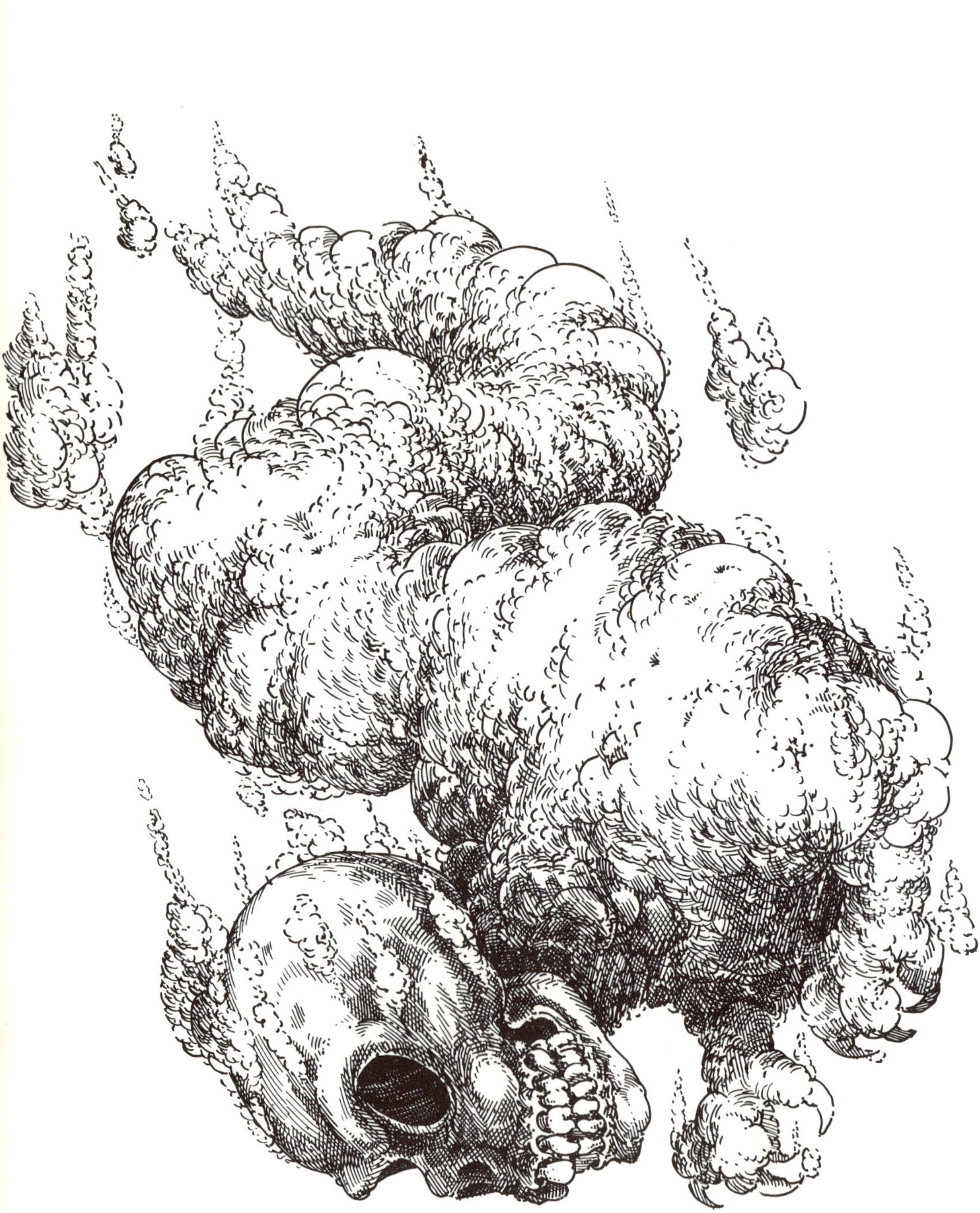

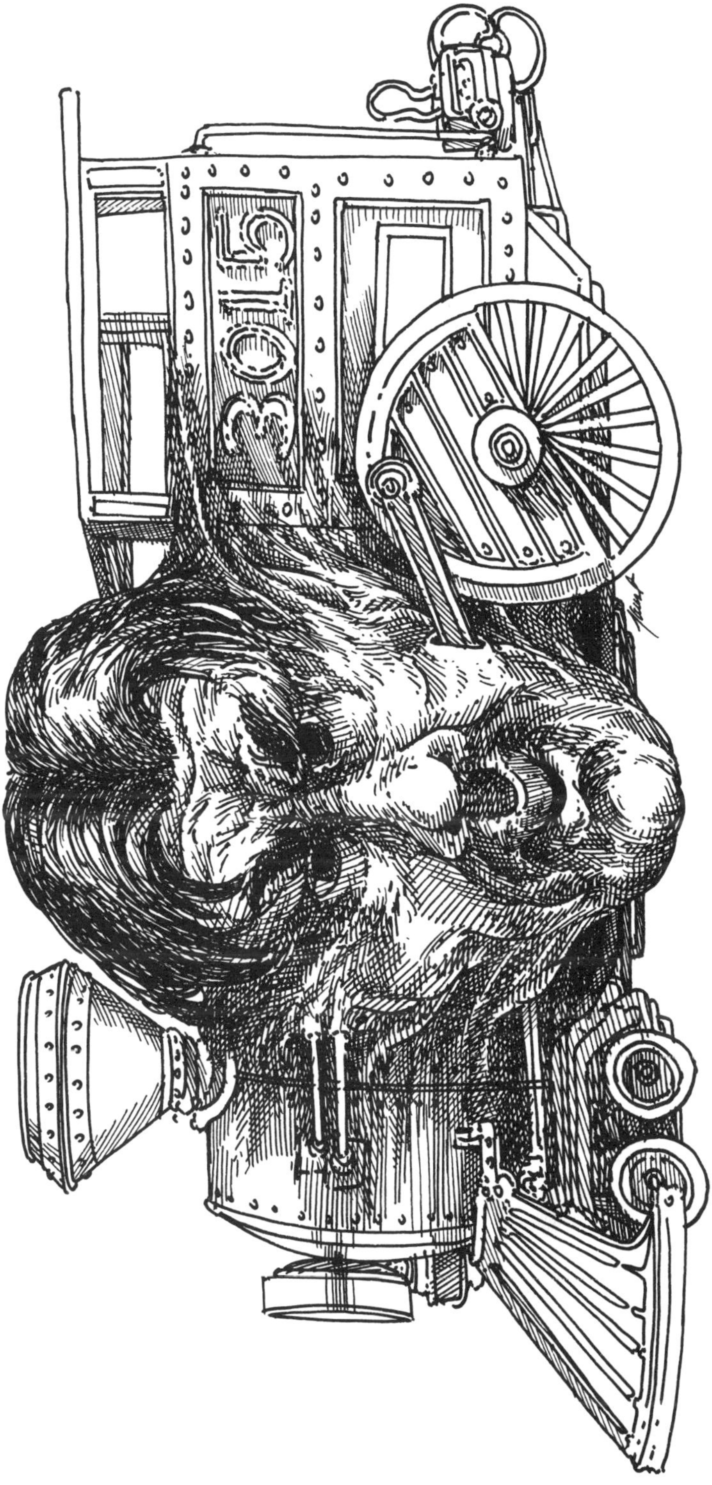

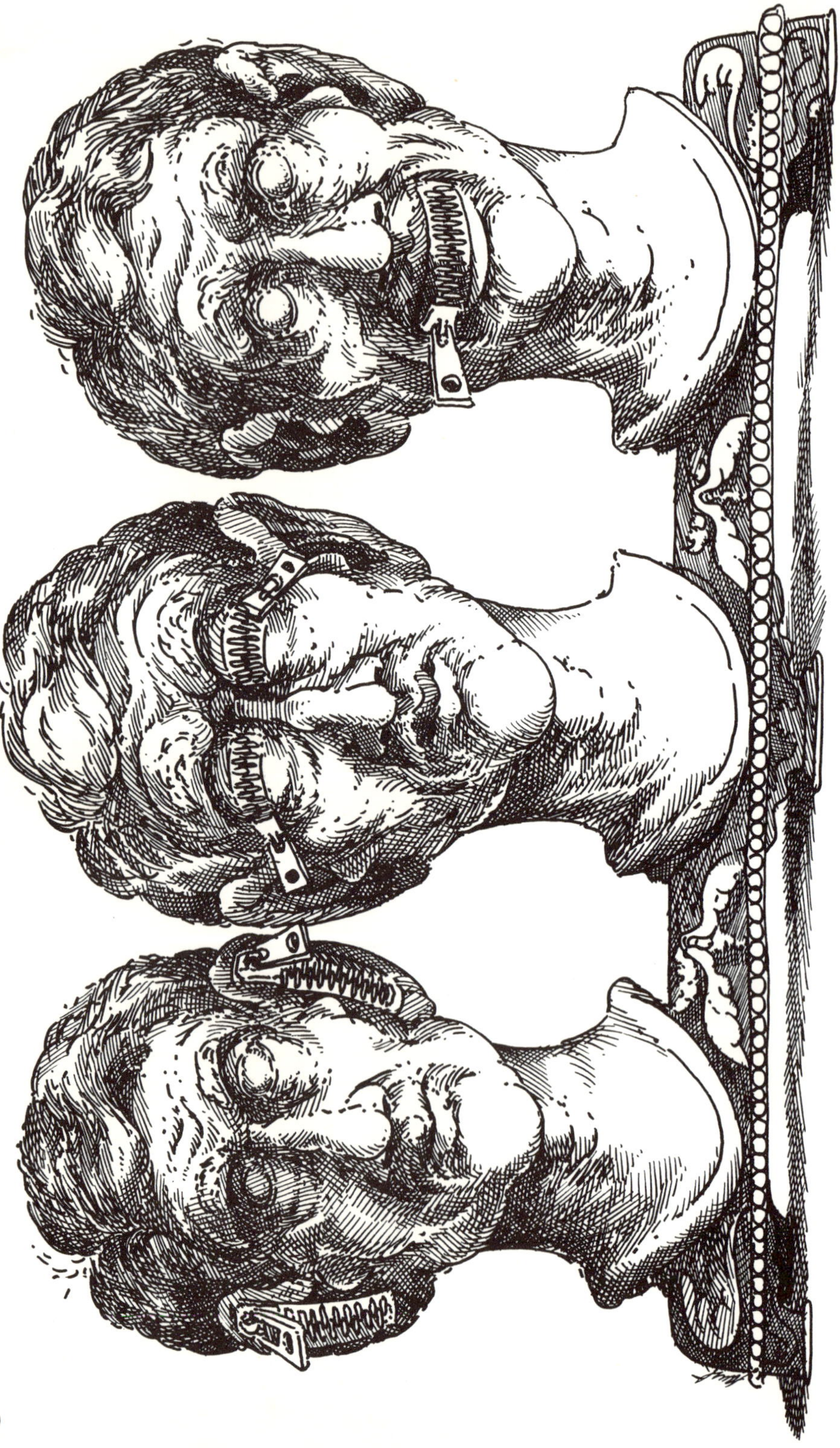

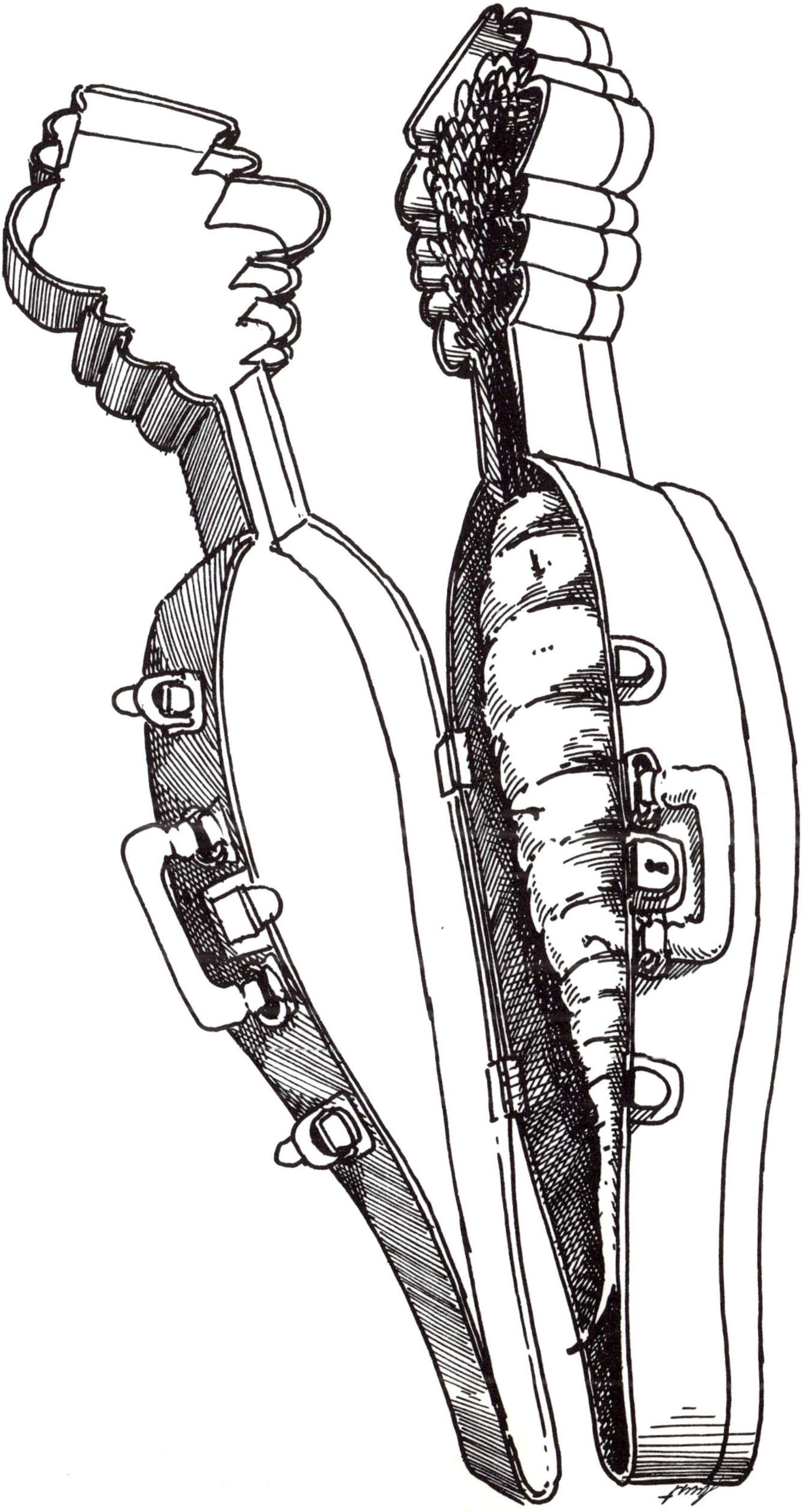

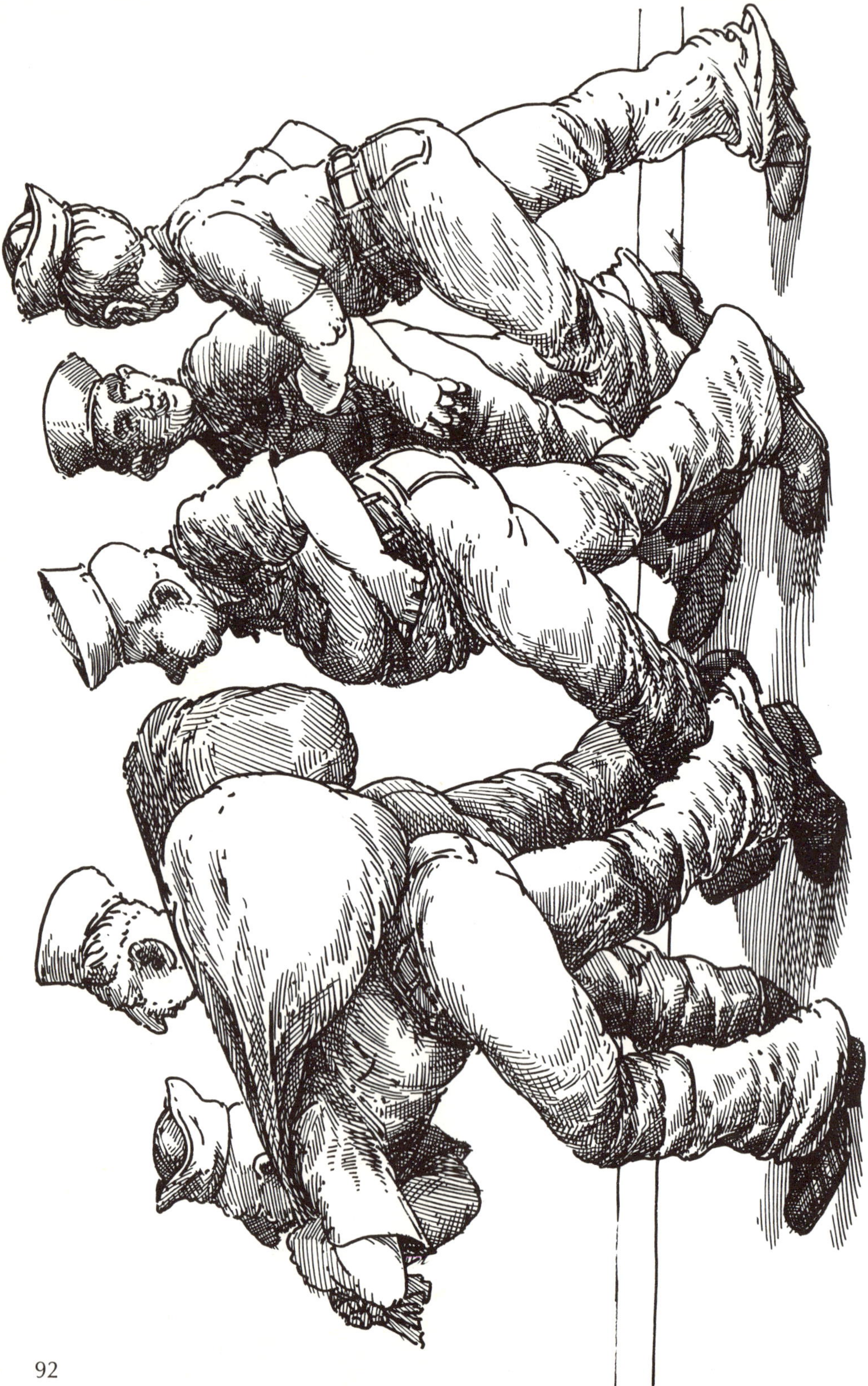

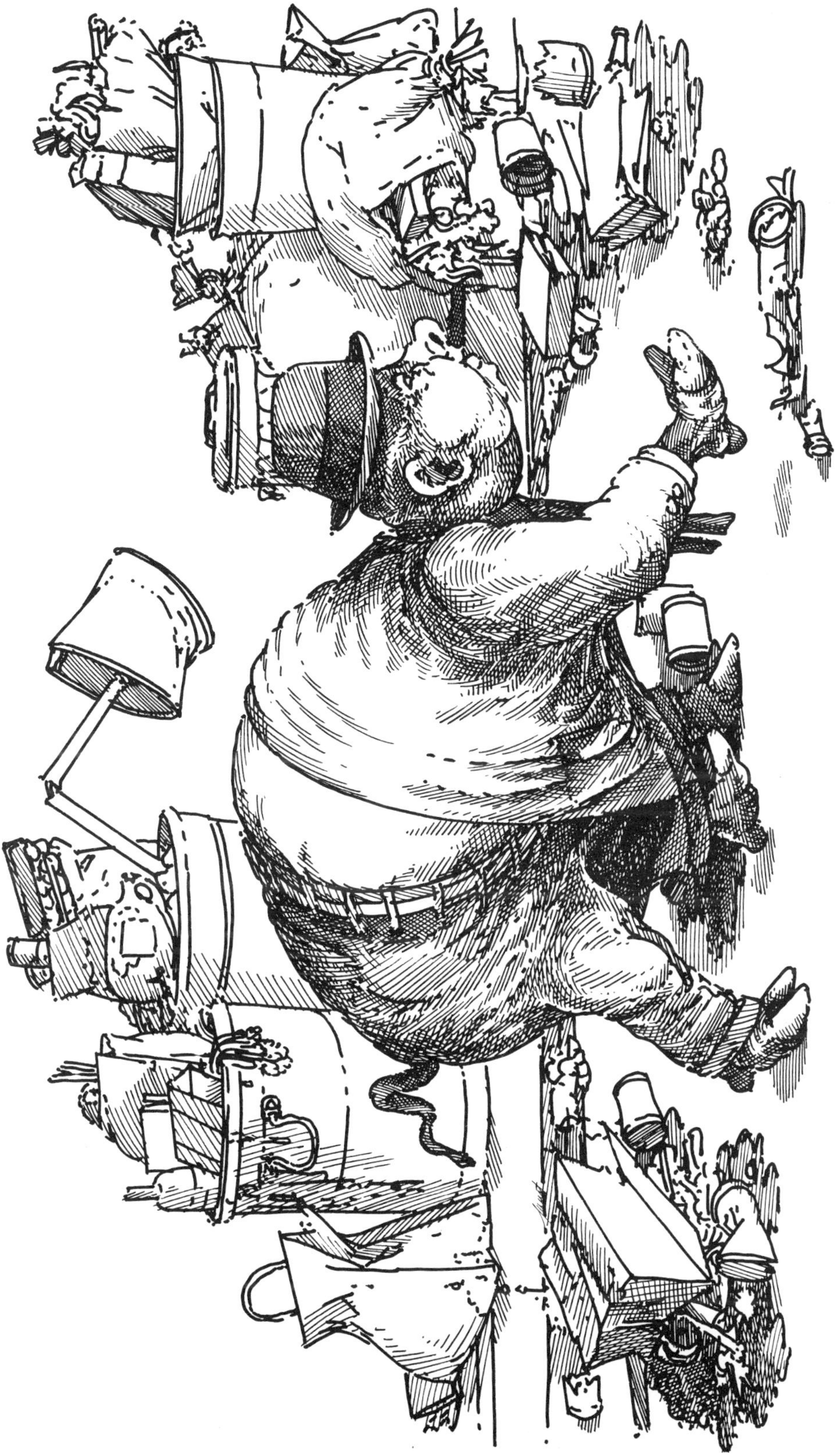

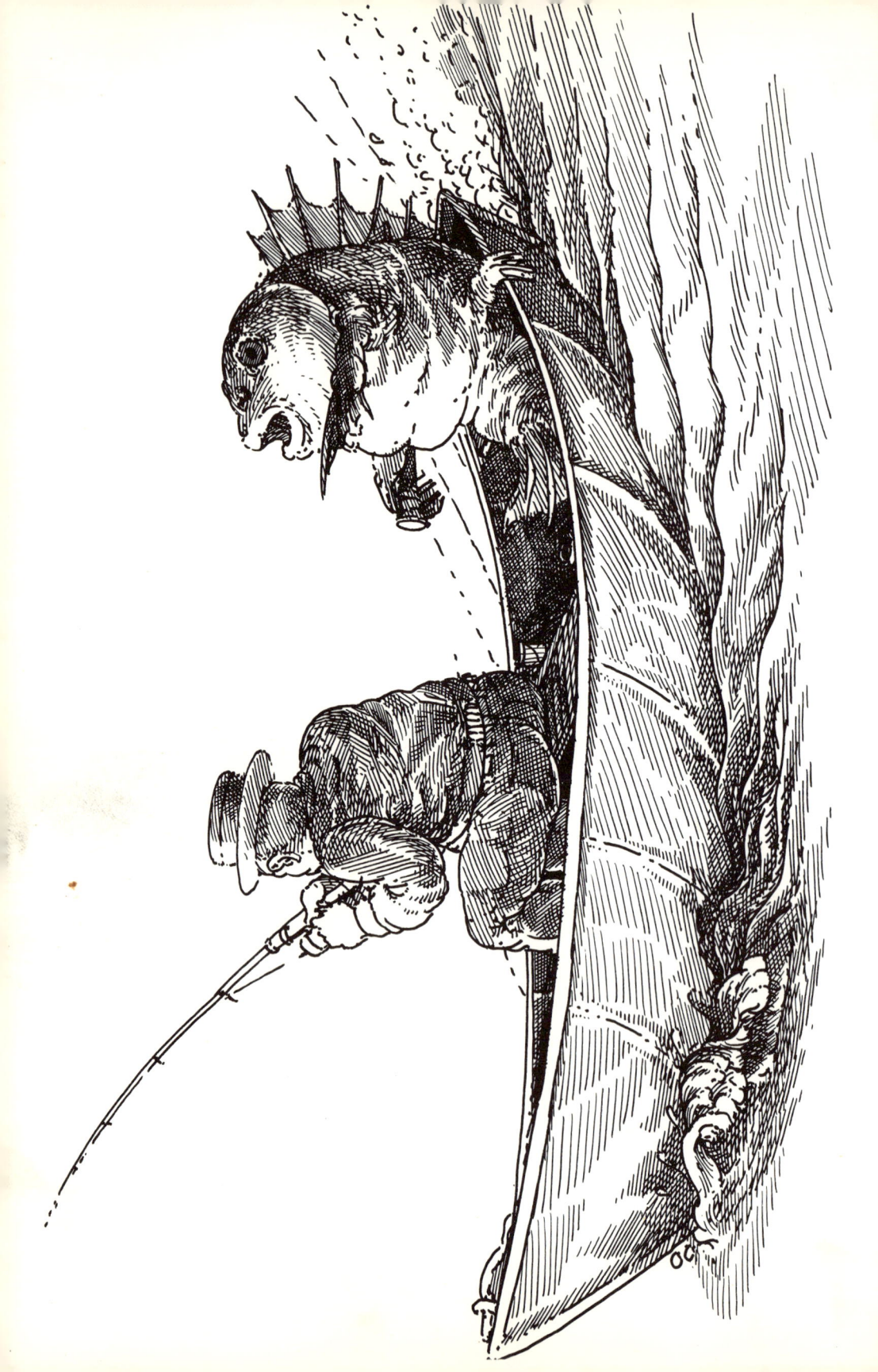

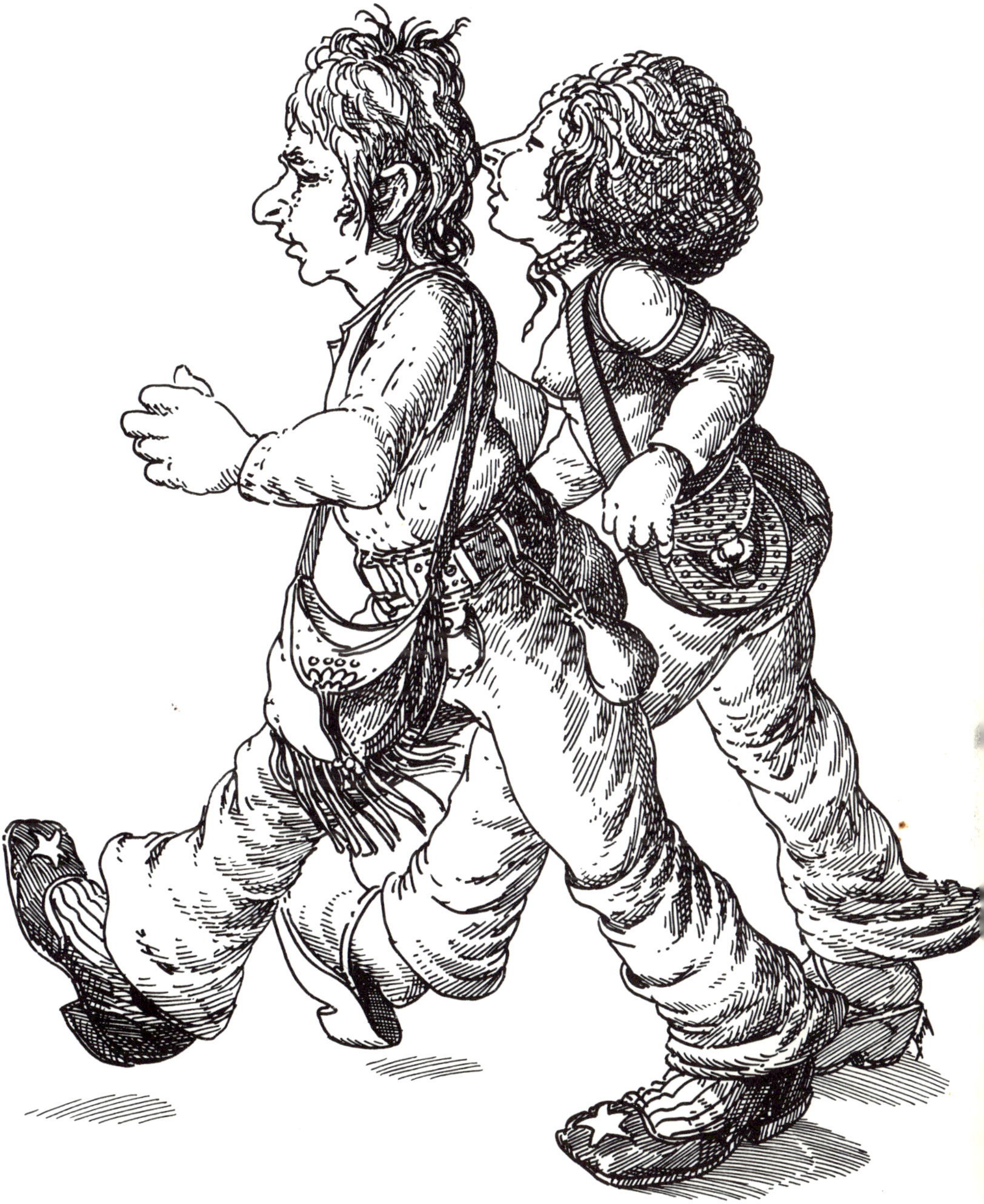

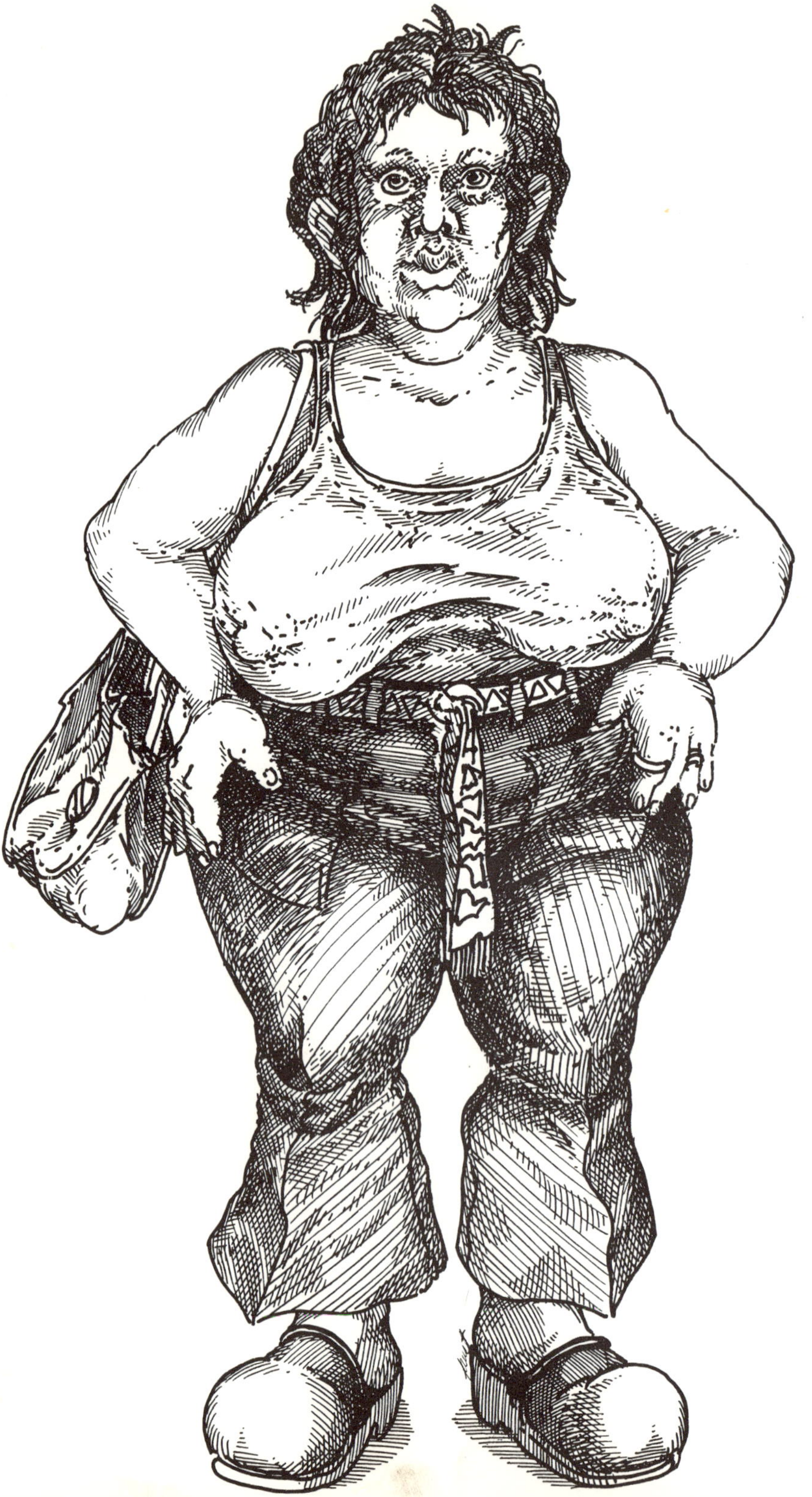

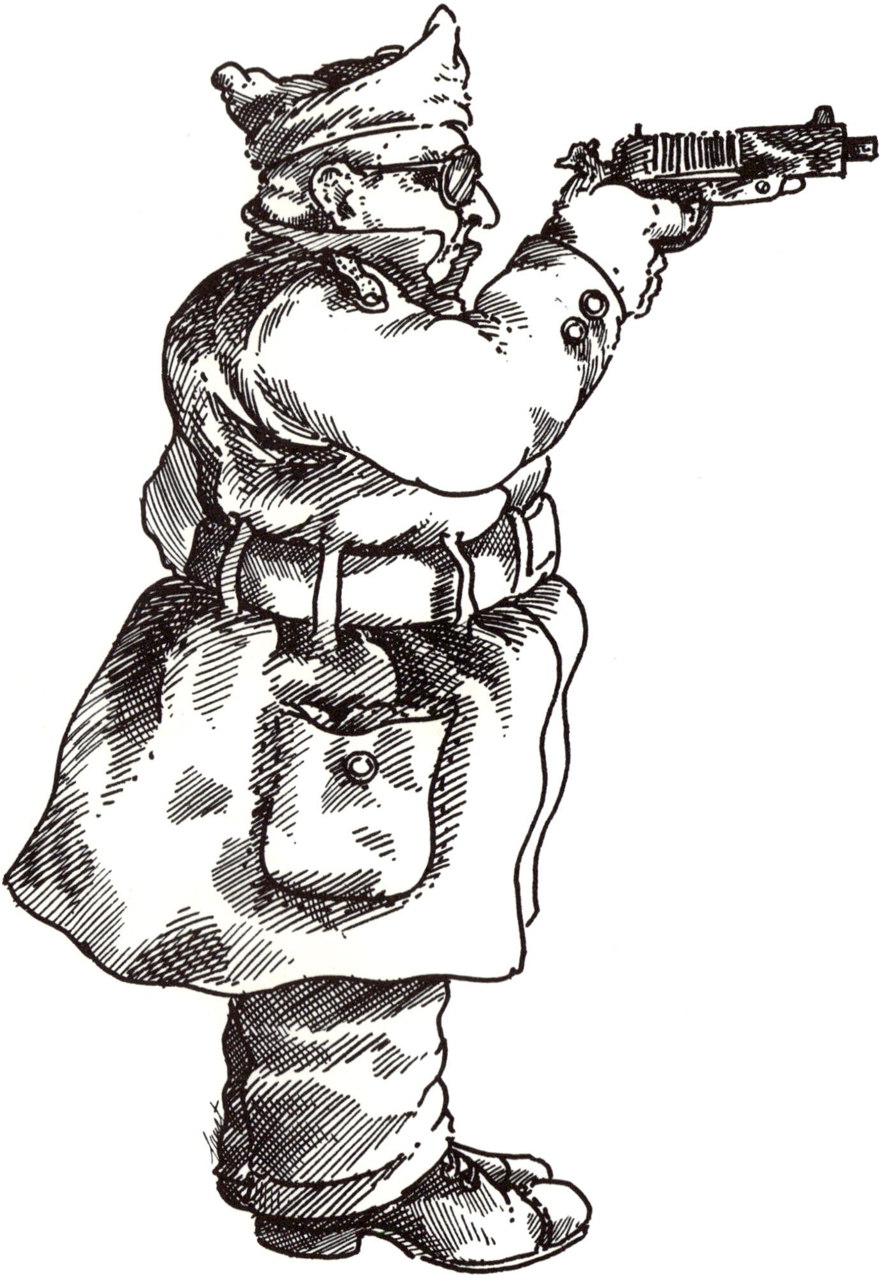

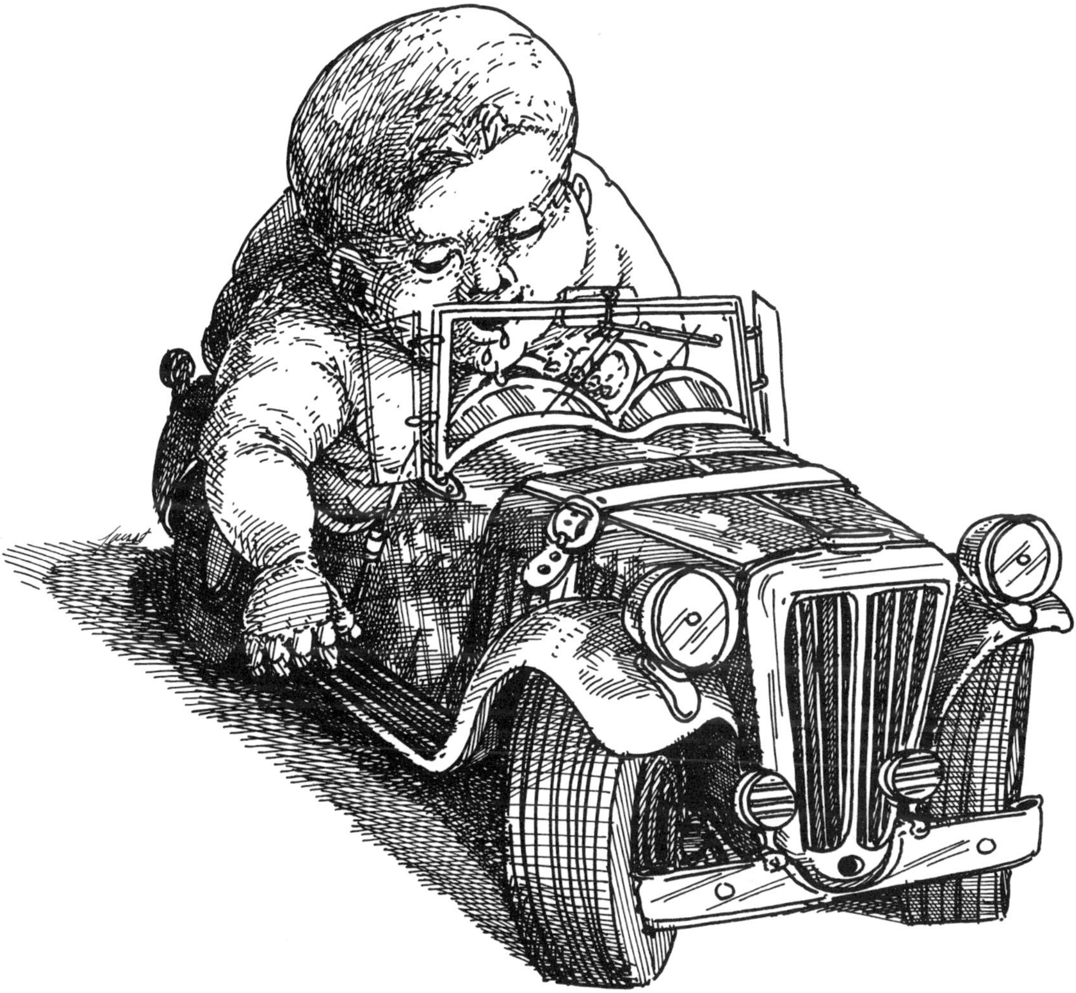

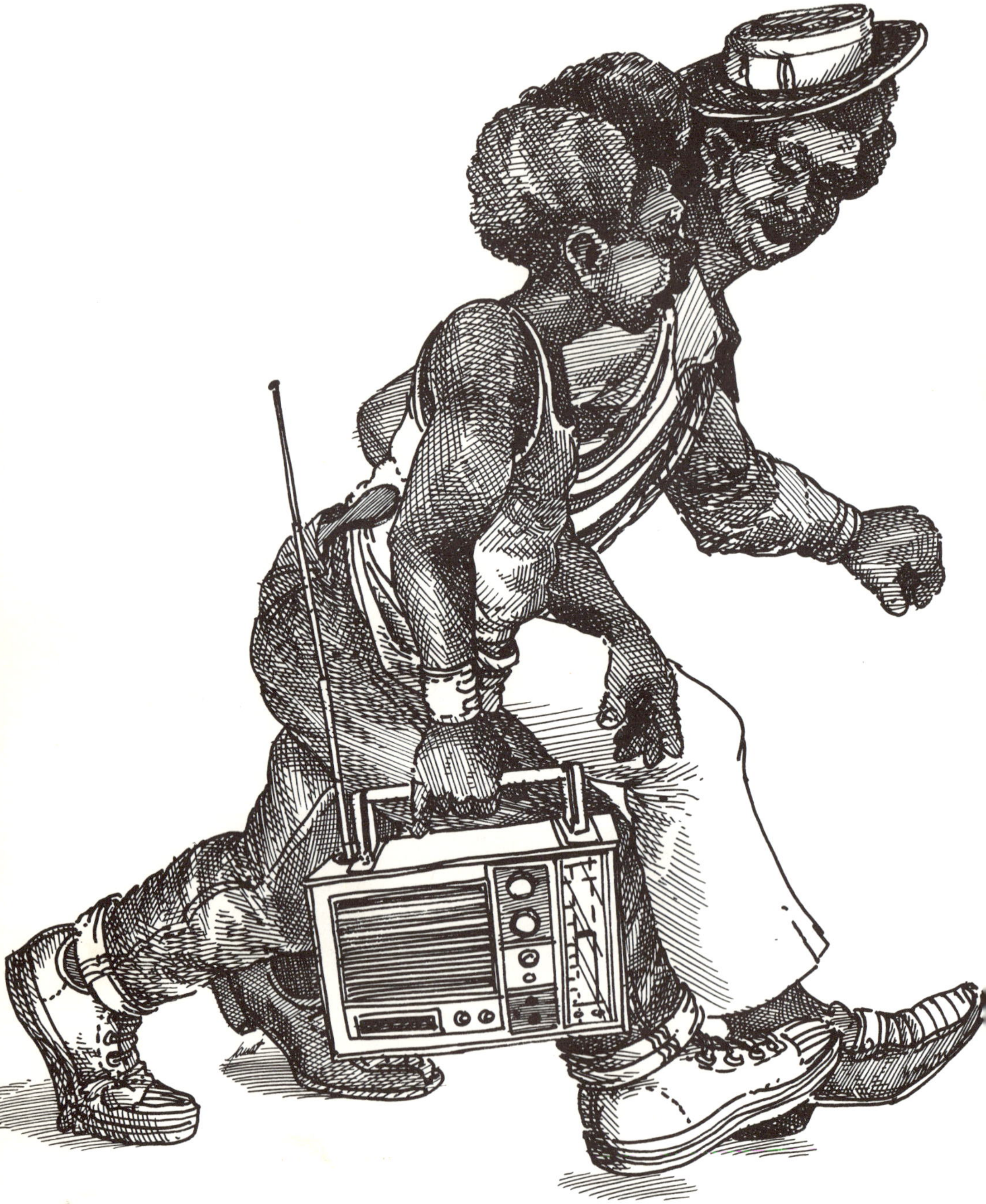

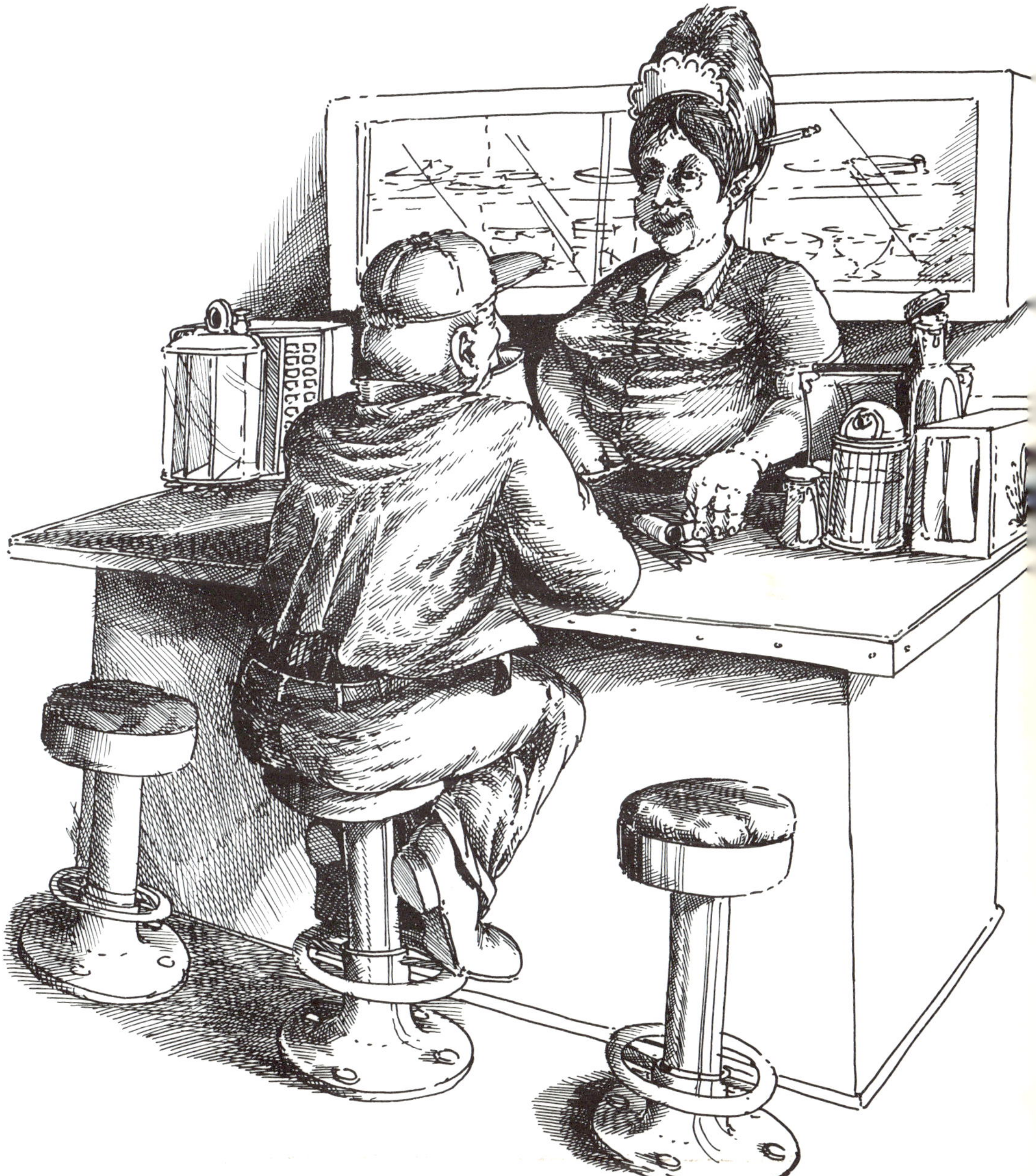

DATE DUE